ALI HAMMUDA

THE FOUR IMAMS

ADAPTED BY:
ZIMARINA SARWAR

The Four Imams

First Published in 2024 by
THE ISLAMIC FOUNDATION

Distributed by
KUBE PUBLISHING LTD
Tel +44 (0)1530 249230
E-mail: info@kubepublishing.com
Website: www.kubepublishing.com

Author Ali Hammuda; adapted by Zimarina Sarwar
Illustration and Book Design by Martha Antonelli
Cover design by Arash Jahani
Art Direction Iman Anwar

A Cataloguing-in-Publication Data record for this book is available from the British Library

ISBN: 978-0-86037-948-5
eISBN: 978-0-86037-953-9

Printed by: Elma Basim, Turkey

THE FOUR IMAMS

By Ali Hammuda
Adapted by Zimarina Sarwar

Kube Publishing

For my father, Said Sarwar

Words of gratitude alone are inadequate to recompense your love, support and strength every day of my life.

Instead, I ask Allāh to enshroud you in His Love always.

Ameen.

Zimarina

Contents

Learn from the best people available to you
Things will come to you at the right time
The purpose of knowledge is action and growth
The benefits of collaboration
Never write people off as a lost cause

Being taught patience from a thief
Forgiven and forgotten?
The death of Imam Ahmad

Introduction

Who are the most important people in your life?

Many of us have family, friends and role models that we look up to, people who inspire us to achieve great things and become better versions of ourselves.

Teachers help us master different subjects and skills, coaches help us train in sports we love, and all of them deserve our appreciation. Of all the people we look up to, there is one particular group that we owe a huge amount to, but we may not even realise why. These people dedicated their lives to learning and teaching, and we benefit from their efforts every day. Who are they? **These are the scholars of Islam.** Scholars spent their lives studying, researching and leaving behind their work for us to understand our life's purpose. But who exactly were these dedicated individuals who worked endlessly to preserve the knowledge of Islam, so we can receive it today?

There have been countless scholars - male and female - throughout history, upholding the religion in every age and era of human civilisation. **Fuelled by sincerity and passion, scholars have emerged in every corner of the world to study and bring our tradition to life.** Of them all however, there are four particular Imams whose legacies have endured the test of time, and who forever remain some of the most important people for us to learn about.

These Four Imams were humans like you and me, they had their own personalities, backgrounds, family histories, personal interests, customs and cultures.

They all went through completely unique and drastically different life events too. What unites all the scholars however is that **their life mission was to uphold and protect the authentic teachings of the Qur'an and Sunnah, and benefit all of humanity** through these precious gifts. These scholars studied deeply and extensively to give us access to the complete, balanced and authentic Sunnah. They learnt to comprehend the big questions around life, death and the universe, as well as routine matters of day-to-day life such as the etiquettes of eating, drinking and sleeping. Because all knowledge was treated as important and precious; these Four Imams enable us to understand Islam in a deep, enriching and holistic way.

These men are not just important historical figures, their important contributions directly impact how we live our lives today. Through learning about the Four Imams, we can imagine what's possible for us to achieve in our own lives. We can learn lessons from the different situations they found themselves in, especially how they responded every time they were confronted with circumstances they didn't expect. We can also learn about what brings true meaning, joy and contentment in life, even if that life takes many twists and turns in our journey through it.

We will learn that these extraordinary people are part of our legacy. Their vision for life is our shared vision. Their goal in life is our shared goal. To know where we are going, we must understand where we came from, and have pride in our Ummah. **These Four Imams are part of you, your intellectual heritage, and your identity as a Muslim.** So let us dive deep and get to know these giants of our history.

Welcome to The Four Imams...

Who were the Four Imams?

Imam Abū Hanīfah
80 AH-150 AH (699 CE-767 CE)

Imam Mālik
93 AH-179 AH (711 CE-795 CE)

Imam al-Shāfiʿī
150 AH-204 AH (767 CE-820 CE)

Imam Aḥmad
164 AH-241 AH (780 CE-855 CE)

Relationship between the Four Imams

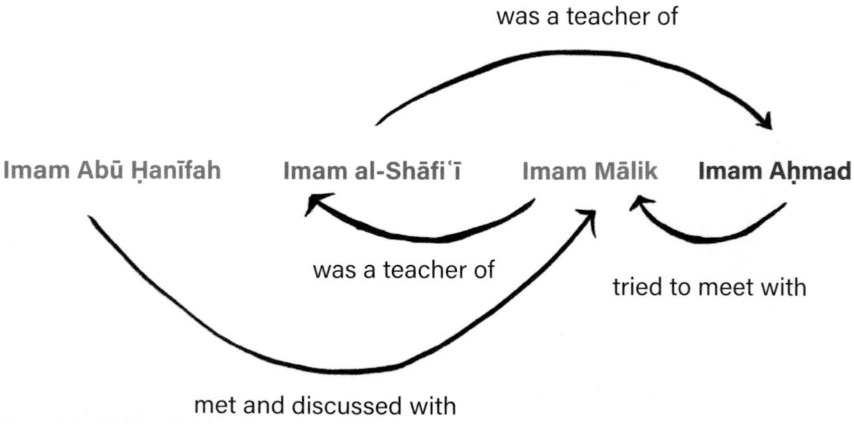

Where were they from?

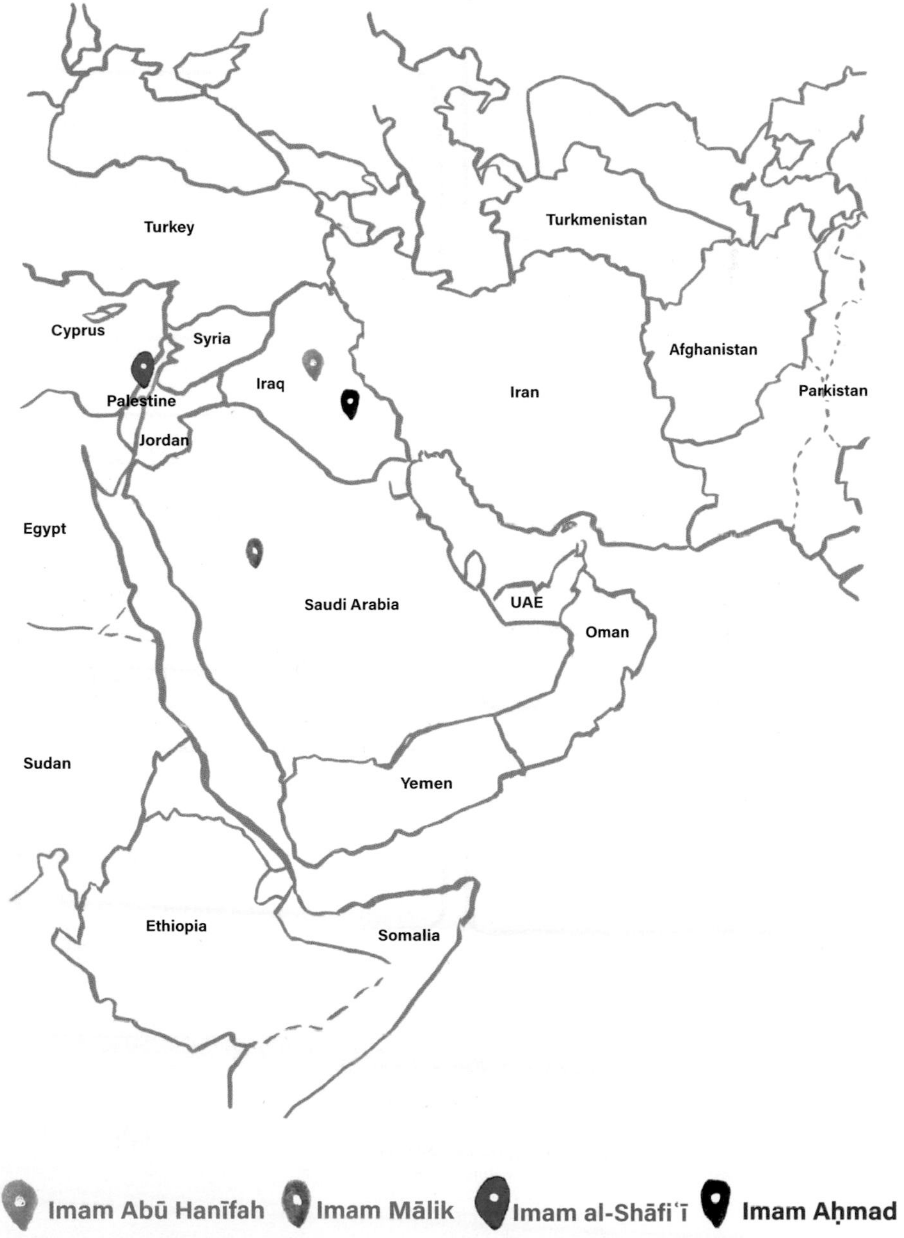
Turkey
Turkmenistan
Cyprus
Syria
Afghanistan
Iraq
Iran
Palestine
Parkistan
Jordan
Egypt
Saudi Arabia
UAE
Oman
Sudan
Yemen
Ethiopia
Somalia
Imam Abū Hanīfah
Imam Mālik
Imam al-Shāfiʿī
Imam Aḥmad

What the Four Imams said about one another

Imam al-Shāfiʿī said about **Imam Abū Ḥanīfah:** *"Every student of fiqh is dependent upon* ***Abū Ḥanīfah.*** *No woman has ever given birth to a man who was wiser than* ***Abū Ḥanīfah."*** [1]

Abū Ḥanīfah was asked about the kind of personality he thought **Imam Mālik** had. **Abū Ḥanīfah** said, *"I debated hundreds of men, but I have never seen a man accept the truth as fast as him."* [3]

After a debate between **Imam Abū Ḥanīfah** and **Imam Mālik,** Imam Mālik wiped his sweat and said: *"By the Almighty,* ***Abū Ḥanīfah*** *made me sweat. By the Almighty, he is a true jurist. I have never seen a man debate like that. By the Almighty, if he told you that this pillar is made out of gold, he would convince you."* [2]

Isḥāq ibn Rahwayh said: ***"Aḥmad ibn Ḥanbal*** *met me in Makkah and said: 'Come here. Let me show you a man the likes of whom your eyes have never seen.' He then showed me* ***al-Shāfiʿī."*** [4]

Imam al-Shāfiʿī said: *"If the scholars are mentioned, then* ***Mālik*** *is the star."* [5]

Imam Aḥmad said: *"There isn't anyone who has touched a pen or paper except that* ***al-Shāfiʿī*** *has virtue over them for it."* [6]

---

[1] Badr al-Din al-'Ayni, *Maghani al-Akhyar fi Sharh Asami Rijal Ma'ani al-Athar,* Dār al-Kutub al-'Ilmīyah, 2006, Vol. 3, p 135 and p 138.

[2] Ibn Ḥajar al-Haythamī, *Al-Khayrat al-Hisān Fi Manāqib al-Imam al-A'zam Abū Ḥanīfah al-Nu'mān Kitab,* Matba'at al-Sa'adah, 1908, p 44.

[3] Imam Shams al-Din al-Dhahabī, *Manāqib al-Imam Abū Ḥanīfah,* Vol 1, p10.

[4] Imam Abu Nu'aym al-Asbahani, *Hilya al-Awliyā',* Dār al-Kutub al-'Ilmīyah, Vol 9, p 97.

Imam Aḥmad ibn Ḥanbal said: *"Had it not been for* ***al-Shāfiʿī,*** *we would not have known the understanding of hadith."* [7]

Imam al-Shāfiʿī said: *"When I left Baghdad, I did not leave behind anyone who was more religiously cautious, pious and scholarly than* ***Aḥmad ibn Ḥanbal."*** [9]

Imam al- Shāfiʿī said: ***"Aḥmad*** *is an Imam in eight matters:*

1. An Imam in Hadith,
2. An Imam in Fiqh,
3. An Imam in Language,
4. An Imam in the Qur'an,
5. An Imam in Poverty,
6. An Imam in Ascetism,
7. An Imam in being Cautious,
8. And an Imam in the Sunnah." [10]

When **Imam Aḥmad's** son asked his father: *"Father, what type of person was* ***al-Shāfiʿī****? I hear you making so much duʿa for him."* **Imam Aḥmad** replied: *"Son,* ***al-Shāfiʿī*** *was like what the sun is for the world, and like what wellbeing is for the body. Can there be a replacement for either?"* [12]

Imam al-Shāfiʿī said: *"Never have I felt greater reverence towards anyone as I did towards* ***Mālik*** *when I saw him."* [8]

Imam al-Shāfiʿī said: *"People are all dependent on* ***Abū Ḥanīfah*** *in fiqh ... and on* ***Mālik*** *in hadith..."* [11]

---

[5] Muḥammad ibn Muḥammad Ḥaṭṭāb, *Mawāhib al-Jalīl li-Sharḥ Mukhtaṣar Khalīl,* Maktabat al-Najāḥ, 1969, Vol 1, p 24.
[6] Ibn ʿAsākir, *Tārīkh Dimashq,* Dār al-Kutub al-'Ilmīyah, 2012, Vol 51, p 349.
[7] Ibn Hajr al-'Asqalani, *Tawālī al-Ta'sīs li Ma'ālī Muḥammad ibn Idrīs,* Dār al-Kutub al-Ilmīyah, 1986, p 96.
[8] Al-Qādi 'Iyād, *Tartib al-Madarik wa Taqrib al-Masalik,* Dār al-Kutub al-'Ilmīyya, 1997, Vol 2, p 34.
[9] Ibn ʿAsākir, *Tārīkh Dimashq,* Dār al-Kutub al-'Ilmīyah, 2012, Vol 5, p 272.
[10] Ibn Abi Ya'la, *Tabaqāt al-Ḥanābilah,* Dār al-Marefah, Beirut, 2004, Vol 1, p 5.
[11] Ibn Hajr al-'Asqalani, *Tahdhib al-Tahdhib,* Mu'assasat al-Resalah, Beirut. p 450.
[12] Ibn al Jawzī, *Ṣifat al-Ṣafwa,* Dār al-Ghad al-Jadeed, Vol 1, p 435.

Imam Abū Ḥanīfah

1

Full name: Al-Nuʿmān son of Thābit son of Zūṭā son of Marzubān

Born in: Kufa, Iraq – 80 AH/699 CE

Died in: Baghdad, Iraq – 150 AH/767 CE (lived for 68 years)

Best known works: *Al-Fiqh al-Akbar, Al-Fiqh al-Absaṭ, Kitāb al-Āthār, Al-ʿĀlim wa'l-Mutaʿallim, Al-Ṭarīq al-Aslam Musnad*

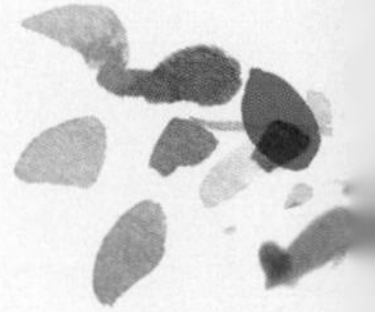

Sweet Beginnings

On a pleasant Spring afternoon in the city of Kufa, a young Thābit closed his fabric shop for the day and began his short walk home. As a textile merchant, Thābit spent his days dealing with the finest silks and exotic fabrics. While planning his next trade mission in his head, a plump and juicy fruit caught his eye and stopped him in his tracks. The tree was full of the season's fruit and though it was in somebody else's garden, Thābit couldn't help but pluck one off the tree and eat it up with relish.

As he finished, a niggling feeling set in his stomach. Was it guilt? Regret? Thābit began to feel uneasy about taking fruit without permission and told himself he needed to set things right. Nervously approaching the house with the garden, Thābit knocked on the front door and found himself in front of the owner.

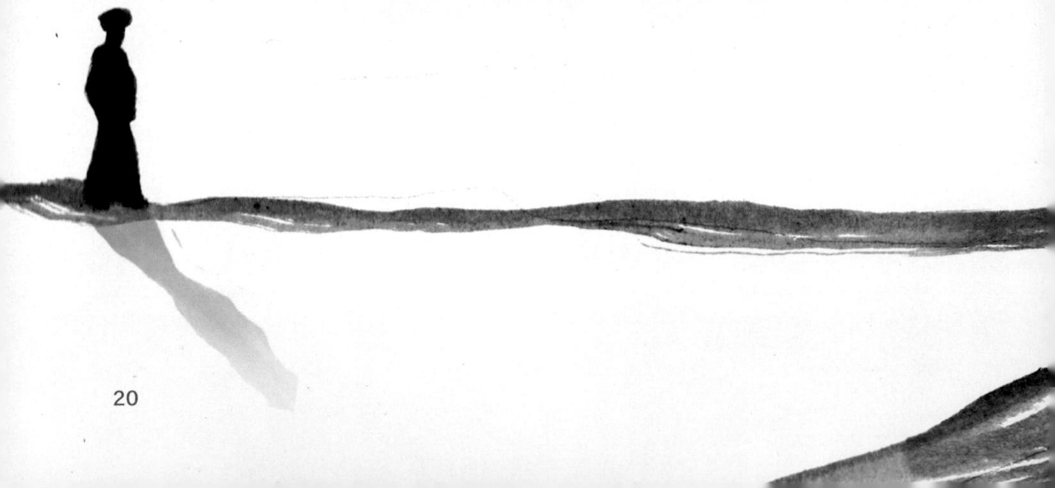

"Young man, what can I do for you?"

"My apologies for disturbing you sir, are you the owner of that fruit tree there?" Thābit cautiously indicated towards the man's orchard.

"Indeed, I am," the man confirmed. *"What can I do for you?"*

Taking a gulp, Thābit explained that he had eaten some fruit without permission and was feeling regretful of his actions, *"I worry that this stolen fruit will be something Allāh will ask me about on the Day of Judgement, please do tell me how I can make it up to you?"*

The owner of the fruit tree listened carefully as Thābit spoke and after a few moments of loaded silence, came up with a deal. *"Well, that tree is one of my favourites and as you've discovered, the fruit from it is very sweet. I will forgive you for taking something that didn't belong to you, only on one condition."*

"Just name it," Thābit assured immediately, *"whatever you wish."*

The man began slowly, *"Very well, to make up for the stolen fruit, I would like you to marry my daughter."*

Thābit's eyes grew wide in surprise, yet he stayed silent as the man was not done. *"In addition, I would like to inform you that my dear daughter is mute, blind, deaf and slow to understand things. Do you agree to this?"*

Thābit fell silent, this was not the afternoon he had anticipated when he closed his fabric shop for the day. However, Thābit was a man of his word, and he really did want to make up for his actions. Without saying a word, he slowly nodded and said, *"Yes sir, I will do that."*

Breaking out into a beaming smile, the man invited Thābit into his house to meet his daughter. The young lady inside greeted her father and his new guest warmly. *"Can I get anything for you both to drink?"* she asked.

Confused, Thābit blurted out, *"But your father told me you were mute, deaf and blind?"* The man's daughter responded graciously, *"Well, I am only deaf from that which is displeasing to Allāh, and I am only mute and blind to that which is forbidden by Allāh, and I am only ignorant of idle knowledge."*

Thābit exhaled as the man extended his hand and said, *"If this was a test of character, you have passed!"*

A short while later, Thābit and the man's daughter were married to both their families' delight. Not long after that, they welcomed a baby boy, named Nuʿmān, into their happy home. This baby, their one and only child, was to become the man the world knows of today as Imam Abū Ḥanīfah. [13]

[13] Abdul-Malik Mujahid, *Gems and Jewels*, Dar-us-Salam Publications, 2004, pp 261-263.

"Abū Ḥanīfah" is a kunyah. What is a *kunyah?*

A *kunyah* in Arabic is the cultural practice of referring to a person by their parent's name (son [ibn]/daughter [bint] of) or their children's name (father [abū]/mother [umm] of). This is considered respectful and honourable.

Not all *kunyahs* are based on people however, sometimes people are named in relation to things that are beloved to them. The close Companion of the Prophet ﷺ, Abū Hurayrah (meaning 'Father of the Kitten') was given that name because he had a kitten he used to play with while herding people's goats for a living.

Similarly, Abū Ḥanīfah was given his name "Father of the Inkpot" as he would carry an inkpot for writing around with him. (Ḥanīfah means ink or inkpot in the Kufic dialect spoken during his time.)

Understanding life in Kufa, Iraq

Alongside Basra and Baghdad, Kufa was one of the three major cities in Iraq at a time where the city was flourishing in Islamic sciences, particularly with people wanting to learn the recitation of the Qur'an. As the Islamic empire was growing rapidly, Imam Abū Ḥanīfah experienced Kufa as a garrison city (that is somewhere where troops are stationed to protect the borders from attack). The people of Kufa were delighted to have the beloved Companion of the Prophet ﷺ Ibn Masʿūd come to help them learn more about their religion and teach in many study circles there.

Because Kufa was on the border of the Islamic Empire, the city became a place that was used to hearing a lot of the ideas about other beliefs and religions. There was a climate of lively discussion and debate in Kufa with many groups competing to have their voices heard. There were ideas from Greek, Roman and Aristotelian philosophy. There were also groups from within the Muslims (the most well-known one called Muʿtazilah) who were challenging basic teachings of Islam.

The Kufa that young Nuʿmān was raised in was a diverse and bustling society, full of ideological discussions. In this way, he witnessed the challenge of living in a time of conflicting beliefs, much like we do today. This intellectual climate no doubt had an impact on Nuʿmān's learning. Diverse opinions can benefit people when people take the good from different sources of learning, but they can also bring a danger if we are not strongly grounded in our own tradition first. Islamic scholarship in Kufa was essential in ensuring Islamic knowledge was kept close to authentic sources, while still tackling opposing ideas being brought forward by others.

During this time, if people wanted to learn about Islam and apply it to their own life, most would look to the scholars from Madinah for advice and guidance. Because most of the Companions of the Prophet ﷺ lived in Madinah and had children there, it was considered the most reliable place to get knowledge on Islamic law (*fiqh*).

What is *fiqh?*

***'Fiqh'* is the Arabic word to describe practical Islamic law.**

When you hear the word 'law', you might think of courts, government or police enforcing the law, but law has a broader meaning than just criminal actions. Islamic law covers day-to-day things for Muslims like the rules of prayer, fasting, giving charity, going on hajj or umrah and even things like inheritance, marriage or what to do during a funeral.

Each of the Four Imams concentrated on *fiqh*, and their own schools of thought gradually developed over time. A school of thought is called a ***madhhab***; this is a methodology to deduce rulings and shows us how to practice Islam in our daily lives.

Early life of young Nuʿmān

All the discussions and debates of Kufa were just background noise for young Nuʿmān as a child, as he was blissfully unaware of anything but helping his father out in his textile business. Nuʿmān learnt a lot about business from an early age, along with how to present himself well with dignified dress. Accompanying his father to work daily taught Nuʿmān a great deal about how to conduct himself in business, and he grew up with a wealth of real-life experience passed on from his very successful father.

When Thābit sadly passed away, his grown son Nuʿmān was fully competent in not only running the family business, but hugely expanding it to become extremely profitable. He inherited 200,000 dirhams from his father. This was considered a huge fortune since – at that time – one could purchase a whole sheep for only 3 dirhams! Of all this money, young Nuʿmān only kept 4000 dirhams for himself and gave himself an allowance of only 2 dirhams a month to spend on himself. He still wore fine clothes as he had access to this through his work and showed that a humble lifestyle can still be one of dignity and honour.

Though Nuʿmān was one of the wealthiest people in his community, he held tight to the principles of charity and fair conduct that his father had taught him. When he had his own child, he would hand his son 10 coins to give to the poor every day and increased this to 20 coins on a Friday.

When he loaned people money, he would never pester them to pay him back. There was once an incident where a man had borrowed money from Nuʿmān and could not afford to pay it back. The man was so worried about his debt, that every time he saw Nuʿmān in the marketplace, he would run and hide from him out of shame. When Nuʿmān came to hear about this, he was shocked and saddened that the man felt he had to do this, and immediately asked the man's forgiveness for making him feel the way that he had. The easy-going nature of Nuʿmān is what made him stand out in his community, long before he began a path to learning Islamic sciences.

Even by today's standards, Nuʿmān is somebody that would be considered very rich. He could afford to live the most lavish lifestyle, own the most luxurious homes and feast on the finest foods available. Nuʿmān, however, had a different approach to wealth. He understood that after your own needs are met, the best use of your blessings is to improve the lives of others around you.

When dealing in business transactions, Nuʿmān was very careful about how he treated customers, and did not take any risks when he was unsure. Once he asked his business partner to sell an item of clothing that was worth 30,000 dirhams. The item had a defect in it and Nuʿmān gave clear and strong instructions to make sure this was shown to the buyer beforehand.

Once the item was sold and the buyer had long departed, his partner confessed that he had forgotten to show the defect to the buyer before he bought the clothing. Upon hearing this, Nuʿmān took the entire 30,000 dirhams and donated it to charity, not wanting to profit from any of it. [14] This incident demon-

[14] Ibn Ḥajar al-Haythamī, *Al-Khayrāt al-Ḥisān Fi Manaqib al-Imam al-A'zam Abī Ḥanīfah al-Nu'mān Kitab,* Matba'at al-Sa'adah, 1908, p 59.

strates everything about the attitude of caution and honesty Nuʿmān applied through his life.

Principles in Business The Abū Ḥanīfah way

It is often said you can tell a lot about a person by observing how they conduct themselves in business. Here were some of the principles Abū Ḥanīfah implemented:

- Never charge or receive interest in business.
- Never take the name of Allāh in an oath to boast how good a product is.
- Never increase prices on customers without a strong reason.
- Never sell a defective product or try to cover up faults.

Dignity in independence

Working in business taught Nuʿmān many things, one of the most important lessons was to always strive to be financially independent. Earning your own living and having the satisfaction that you can afford to support yourself is an important part of life and all the scholars of Islam encouraged this greatly.

The Prophet ﷺ even said: *"Nobody has eaten a better meal than that which one has earned by working with one's own hands, and the Prophet of Allāh, David, would eat from the earnings of his manual labour."* [15]

We have a rich and fascinating history of the kinds of jobs that our great scholars did to earn an income, alongside their studies and teaching. They showed how we can excel not only in matters of our religion, but also excel when it comes to our jobs and livelihood. [16]

---

[15] Al-Bukhārī, *Sahih al-Bukhārī*, Mohee Uddin, 2020, Vol 3, p 57.

[16] Abdul Bāsit b. Yūsuf al-Gharīb, *Al-Turfa fī man Nusiba min al-ʿUlamāʾi ilā Miḥnah aw Ḥirfah.*

The Many Jobs of Scholars

Al-Zajjaj
The Glassmaker

Al-Qaffal
The Locksmith

Al-Najjar
The Carpenter

Al-Haddad
The Blacksmith

Al-Bazzaz
The Draper

Al-Attar
The Perfume Seller

Al-Qassab
The Sugar Cane Worker

Al-Jassas
The Plasterer

Al-Khabbaz
The Baker

Earning your own honest living is an idea embedded within the Sunnah of our Prophet ﷺ who encouraged people to work hard for themselves and their families.

The Messenger of Allāh ﷺ said: *"No doubt, it is preferable that you gather a bundle of wood and carry it on your back (to earn your living) than ask somebody who may give (you what you need) or not."* [17]

[17] Al-Bukhārī, *Sahih al-Bukhārī,* Mohee Uddin, 2020, Vol 3, p 57.

A few short words pave the way

As a wealthy young man, life was great for Nuʿmān. He was kept busy in his trade and was a loved and trusted member of his community because of his generous character. On a day much like any other, Nuʿmān was stopped by a special kind of passer-by. The scholar al-Shaʿbī spotted young Nuʿmān in a crowd and pulled him aside swiftly, asking, *"Who do you visit?"* A little taken aback, Nuʿmān replied, *"I'm going ... to the marketplace?"* to which al-Shaʿbī replied, *"I do not mean that. I meant to ask, who among the scholars do you visit?"*

"I do not visit them much," came the honest answer from Nuʿmān. With concern, al-Shaʿbī advised, *"Do not behave thoughtlessly, rather turn to knowledge and the circles of scholars, because I see alertness and energy in you."*

Reflecting on this brief exchange, Imam Abū Ḥanīfah later said, *"The love of what he said was placed in my heart, so I left the marketplace and turned to knowledge. Allāh benefitted me a great deal through his advice."* [18]

With this vote of confidence, Nuʿmān found motivation to seek out the scholars of Kufa and begin his path to gaining Islamic knowledge. Because of his keen intellect and curious nature, Nuʿmān's initial interest in Islamic learning was in the science of *Kalām.*

What is Kalām?

***'Kalām'* means to study the way Islamic theological issues are understood and spoken about.** It can involve sharing, debating and discussing with others who have different perspectives. These conversations use philosophy and logic to discuss religious questions.

Kalām is one of many sciences within Islamic learning. Others include:
- ***Sīrah*** (the study of the life of the Prophet ﷺ).
- ***Tafsīr*** (the commentary on the Qur'an).
- ***Fiqh*** (the practical law and rules of Islam).
- ***Tazkiyah*** (the study of purifying your soul).

Now officially a student of knowledge, Nuʿmān became known as Imam Abū Ḥanīfah. Though he was only 20 years old at the time, he soon became extremely prominent for his skills in debate and discussion. He travelled over twenty-seven times from his home city on long journeys to Baghdad, specially to meet with people for debate. He defended the authentic teachings of Islam from people trying to introduce inaccurate and faulty ideas into it. Unfortunately, there were many individuals and groups who – for their own reasons – were trying intentionally to change the religion and subvert the message of Islam. At such a time in Kufa, with many new philosophies and ideas taking root, Abū Ḥanīfah was kept very busy in his role.

[18] Muhammad ibn Ahmad ibn Ismail Muqaddam, *'Uluww al-Himmah,* Dar al-Iman, 2004, Vol 8, p 11.

When the path to knowledge takes a detour

Just as Imam Abū Ḥanīfah had become known all over Iraq for his powerful intellect and strong understanding, something happened to drastically change the course of his studies. While teaching a large group of students one day, a woman in the audience raised her hand and asked a simple question about divorce. Completely lost for an answer, Imam Abū Ḥanīfah told her to go to the class of another teacher - Ḥammād ibn Abī Sulaymān - and get the answer from him. He also asked her to report the answer back to him when she got it. When the woman did so, Imam Abū Ḥanīfah openly declared, *"I have lost my interest in Kalām".* With that, he promptly picked up his shoes and sat - as a student - in the circle of the scholar Ḥammād to begin studying *fiqh.*

A student-teacher relationship like no other

Here in this circle, Imam Abū Ḥanīfah remained for over 18 years. He eagerly absorbed all the knowledge Ḥammād had to offer and served him as a student for almost two decades. Ḥammād recognised that Imam Abū Ḥanīfah wasn't like the average students; he would memorise his teachings word for word whilst others would forget. He had an enthusiasm for learning that his other students simply could not match.

Over time, Abū Ḥanīfah evolved to become more than a student to Ḥammād, but also a friend and personal assistant. He would assist him in carrying his books and groceries, tend to the household and garden of his teacher and take questions from the public and report back. In turn, Ḥammād held Abū Ḥanīfah in such high esteem that he told his other students: *"No one is to sit at the forefront of the study circle next to me except Abū Ḥanīfah."* [19]

In his own words, Imam Abū Ḥanīfah says:

"I accompanied Ḥammād for ten years, then my soul began to yearn for a position of authority. I considered breaking away and starting up my own study circle. On one evening, I made my way to the Masjid with the intention of doing just that, but when I saw Ḥammād, I could not bring myself to do so. During that evening's class, Ḥammād was told that a relative of his had passed away in Basra. This relative had left behind some wealth and Ḥammād was the only inheritor. Before he left, he instructed me to teach in his place.

[19] Abu Bakr Ahmad bin Ali al-Khatib al-Baghdādi
Tahqiq, *Tārīkh Baghdād*, Dār al-Kutub al-'Ilmīyah, Vol 15, p 444.

"Ḥammād left, and so the students asked me questions that I had not heard Ḥammād answer before. I would answer the questions and write down my own answers. After two months, Ḥammād returned. I showed him the questions I was asked and how I answered them. There were around sixty questions. He approved of forty of my answers and disagreed with twenty of them.

"From that day, I vowed to myself I would never leave his side until he passes away." [20]

Ḥammād, however, was not the only teacher of Abū Ḥanīfah, but one of a staggering 4000 teachers; 93 of whom were from the *Tābiʿīn*.

The Prophet ﷺ to Imam Abū Ḥanīfah An Unbroken Chain

The Prophet Muḥammad ﷺ

↓

ʿAbdullāh ibn Masʿūd

↓

ʿAlqamah

↓

Ibrāhīm al-Nakhaʿī

↓

Ḥammād ibn Abī Sulaymān

↓

Imam Abū Ḥanīfah

[20] Abu Bakr Ahmad bin Ali al-Khatīb al-Baghdādi Tahqiq, *Tārīkh Baghdād*, Dār al-Kutub al-'Ilmīyah, Vol 15, p 444.

What is a *Tābi'ī* ?

- The first generation of Muslims are known as the *Sahābah* or the Companions of Muhammad ﷺ.
- The second generation of Muslims who came after the *Sahābah* are called Tābiʿūn in plural and Tābiʿī in singular (which means "the successors").
- The third generation of Muslims coming after the *Tābiʿūn* (who knew at least one Tābiʿī) are called *Tābiʿ al-Tābiʿīn.*

These three generations make up the 'Salaf' (Predecessors) of Islam.

The Prophet Muhammad ﷺ said: *"The best people are those living in my generation (Sahābah: the first generation), then those coming after them (Tābiʿūn: the second generation), and then those coming after (Tābiʿ al-Tābiʿīn: the third generation)."*

Ṣaḥīḥ al-Bukhārī

The character of Imam Abū Ḥanīfah

As well as his commitment to learning, there were many other aspects of Imam Abū Ḥanīfah's character that he was well known for.

Though Abū Ḥanīfah spent a lot of time debating and discussing ideas with people, he never made his discussions personal and was never heard to say a bad word about others. One of Abū Ḥanīfah's students, ʿAbdullāh ibn al-Mubārak, was one day talking about him to his other teacher Sufyān al-Thawrī when he marvelled:

"How distant is Abū Ḥanīfah from making slanderous statements, I have never even heard him backbite his enemies." Sufyān responded, "By Allāh, he is wiser than to allow someone to walk away with his good deeds." [21]

[21] Ibn Khallikān, *Wafayāt al-Aʿyān wa-Anbāʾ Abnāʾ al-Zamān,* Oriental Translation Fund of Great Britain and Ireland, Paris, 1868, Vol 5, p 411.

Abū Ḥanīfah also set strict rules and a higher standard of conduct upon himself that he did not impose on others. This included a condition that he placed upon himself that every time he took an oath using Allāh's name (to say: "I swear by Allāh..."), he would follow this up by donating a dinār in charity. He did this to honour the mention of Allāh's name and to train himself not to casually take oaths in Allāh's name for trivial matters. When Abū Ḥanīfah would spend on his family, for every dinar spent towards his household he donated the same amount to the poor.

He was also cautious about acquiring knowledge but not putting it into practice. He knew that the more you know, the more responsibility you have to act on it. We have been informed in the Sunnah of the importance of seeking knowledge that benefits us. In fact, one of the most regular duʿas of the Prophet ﷺ was:

"Oh Allāh, I seek refuge in You from knowledge that is not beneficial, from a heart that does not humble itself to You, from desire that is not satisfied, and from a prayer that is not answered." [22]

Imam Abū Ḥanīfah was very conscious that if the things you know do not make a real change in your behaviour, manners and worship, then something is wrong and needs to be urgently worked on.

During the evenings, it was common for Abū Ḥanīfah to perform his nightly *'Ishā'* prayer and then stand so long in prayer, that by the time it got to *Fajr* time, he would pray without needing to redo his *wuḍū'.* It is reported that during the summer months, he would only sleep between *Ẓuhr* (noon) and *ʿAṣr* (afternoon) time. During Winter, he would sleep lightly in the first portion of the night while in the mosque.[23]

One of the interesting and unique things about Imam Abū Ḥanīfah was how much he travelled in his lifetime, not only compared to the other Imams, but also considering how much more difficult travelling long distances was in his time. He performed hajj an astonishing fifty-five times in his life. His dedication to worship also included being a close friend of the Qur'an too. Outside of prayer, he would complete the recitation of the Qur'an every three days. He spent much time in contemplation too, and once spent an entire night in prayer repeating one Qur'anic verse over and over again as he wept:

"By the Hour is their appointment, and the Hour is most disastrous and most bitter." [24]

Many say that the arrival of Imam Abū Ḥanīfah was part of a Prophetic prediction. The Prophet ﷺ was once sitting with the Companions and he put his bless-

---

22 Imam Abul-Husain Muslim, *Ṣaḥiḥ Muslim*, Dar-us-Salam Publications Inc, 2007, Vol 4, p 2088.

23. Ibn Abī al-ʿAwām, *Fada'il Abī Ḥanīfah wa Akhbaruhu wa Manaqibuh*, Vol 1, p 58.

24. Al-Dhahabī, *Siyar A'lām al-Nubalā',* Dār al-Kutub al-'Ilmīyah, Vol 6, p 401.

ed arm around Salmān al-Fārsī, the Persian Companion. The Prophet ﷺ said, *"Even if faith was left amongst the stars, a man from the Persians would grab it."* [25] Here, the Prophet ﷺ is predicting a great *mujaddid*, reviver of Islam, to come from Persia. Many interpret this hadith to refer to none other than Imam Abū Ḥanīfah. One can see why then Imam Abū Ḥanīfah was called "The Imam" by Abū Dāwūd, and "The Imam, one of those who have reached the sky" by Ibn Ḥajar and is known in the Islamic world as "The greatest Imam" *(al-Imam al-aʿẓam).*

Imam Abū Hanīfah and the drunk neighbour

At home in Kufa, Imam Abū Ḥanīfah had a neighbour who would spend most of his night drinking and when completely drunk, he would sing the following lines at the top of his voice:

"They have neglected me, but what a man they have neglected! They shall realise their loss at times of war!"

The man was known as a brave fighter, so although people didn't see the man's value now, he was sure they would miss him when, one day, they needed him on the battlefield.

The drunk neighbour would repeatedly sing these lines all night until he exhausted himself and fell asleep. Next door, Imam Abū Ḥanīfah would also be awake, but for very different reasons: his night prayer. All night long, every evening, Imam Abū Ḥanīfah would hear his neighbour's loud singing and try his best to ignore it so he could concentrate on his prayer.

One evening, things were altogether more silent. As Imam Abū Ḥanīfah prepared for his night prayer, he couldn't help but notice the lack of his neighbour's wailing and warbling. Concerned for what might have happened to him, Imam Abū Ḥanīfah immediately began making enquiries about the young man. He was informed that the man had been arrested and imprisoned by the city's police for public drunkenness.

Early the next morning, Imam Abū Ḥanīfah carried out his *Fajr* prayer, mounted his ride and made his way straight to the governor's residence. The governor was overjoyed to receive such a high-status visitor as Imam Abū Ḥanīfah and treated him as an honoured guest. During the meeting, Imam Abū Ḥanīfah asked about his drunken neighbour and requested his release. The governor responded by not only freeing Imam Abū Ḥanīfah's neighbour, but all the other prisoners who had been arrested that night as an act of forgiveness.

---

[25] Imam Abul-Husain Muslim, *Ṣaḥiḥ Muslim,* Dar-us-Salam Publications Inc, 2007, Vol 4, p 1972.

Once his neighbour arrived home, sobered up by a long and cold night in a prison cell, Abū Ḥanīfah approached him to ask, *"Young man, have I neglected you as my neighbour?"* His neighbour replied, *"No, you have preserved and safeguarded me, so may Allāh reward you for being such a good neighbour and guardian of rights."*

This moment became the turning point in the young man's life. He turned to Allāh in repentance and vowed never to go back to his old ways. From that day onwards, his neighbour never touched a drop of alcohol again, and began a productive and fulfilling life. [26]

The *fiqh* of Imam Abū Hanīfah: A collective effort

Students of the Imams often continued to work on their schools of thought for many years, meaning they reached maturity over decades after the Imam passed away. This is the *fiqh* collection of their work and a practical manual we can use for our day-to-day lives. Each Imam was an individual living in his own context and, as a result, there are small differences between each of the schools of thought. The Imams themselves accepted their differences and held one another in high regard without creating divisions or disputing with one another.

One of the features of Imam Abū Ḥanīfah's *madhhab* was that it was formed as a collective effort of a council of extremely knowledgeable people and was not the mere opinions of Imam Abū Ḥanīfah alone. As the head of the council, Imam Abū Ḥanīfah had approximately 36-40 of his students, who were each a master of Islamic sciences from great scholars of *fiqh,* hadith, language and jurisprudence. Some of his most prominent scholars were Muhammad ibn al-Ḥasan, al-Qāḍī Abū Yūsuf, Imam Zufar, and Ḥafṣ ibn Ghiyath.

[26] Abu Bakr Ahmad bin Ali al-Khatīb al-Baghdādi Tahqiq, *Tarīkh Baghdād,* Dār al Kutub al 'Ilmīyah, Vol 15, p 487.

When an issue was being decided, Abū Ḥanīfah had a very particular approach:

- The matter to be discussed *(mas'alah)* would be presented.
- Every participant would be invited to speak on the topic.
- A discussion would take place back and forth (this sometimes lasted over a month!).
- Once the council had decided they had explored the issue fully, they would ask for Imam Abū Ḥanīfah's input.
- Abū Ḥanīfah would share his stance and reconcile this with the strongest opinions of his council.
- Only after everybody had reached a united decision and comfortable consensus, would that opinion be officially recorded as part of the *fiqh* of Imam Abū Ḥanīfah.
- It should be noted not all students always arrived at the same conclusion (differences of opinion are natural!). Not all opinions were a consensus, however everybody understood one another's perspectives deeply and respected them.

One of the great benefits of having such a council of people come together to share their opinions is that you can draw knowledge from a wide variety of backgrounds. Some of the scholars were experts in Qur'an recitation, some were masters of hadith, others had the deepest knowledge of the Arabic language, others were known for being committed to *tazkiyah*, while some were serving as judges in legal courts.

Each of these people were invited to bring the full scope of their wide knowledge together and tackle issues from multiple different angles. With this approach, experts from multiple fields are pooled together to give a balanced and all-round perspective on all the issues being dealt with.

Best of the best:
The students supporting Imam Abū Hanīfah

Earlier we learnt about the devoted relationship Imam Abū Ḥanīfah had with his beloved teacher Ḥammād, however the chain of loyalty did not end there. When Imam Abū Ḥanīfah began leading his own circles of study, he was blessed with students who were active, committed and proactive in supporting the work of their great teacher. Though all the Imams had dutiful students, Imam Abū Ḥanīfah's were considered the ones who most enthusiastically spread his teachings and message as far as they could. Imam Abū Ḥanīfah's two most famous students, al-Qāḍī Abū Yūsuf and Muḥammad al-Shaybānī, went on to develop the Ḥanafī *madhhab* further. The number of books that Imam Abū Ḥanīfah wrote himself are actually very few in number, it was his students who took on the privilege and responsibility of presenting the *fiqh* of their much-loved teacher throughout the world.

When Wakīʿ heard a person saying: "Imam Abū Ḥanīfah made a mistake," he responded: "How can he make a mistake when with him are the likes of Abū Yūsuf and Zufar who are known for their *Qiyās*; Yaḥyā b. Abī Zā'idah, Ḥafṣ ibn Ghiyāth, Ḥibbān, and Mandal, all of whom are known for their memorization of hadith; Al-Qāsim b. Maʿn who is known for his knowledge of the Arabic language; and Dāwūd al-Ṭā'ī and al-Fuḍayl b. ʿIyāḍ who are known for their *Zuhd* (piety) and caution? Whoever has such people as his companions will rarely make mistakes, because if he does, they will correct him." [27]

Whilst Abū Ḥanīfah was pioneering with his *fiqh* council, he would not hide behind the group if an issue could not be solved. Rather, he took responsibility for this himself. If a matter remained unclear to Abū Ḥanīfah, struggling to reach a conclusive opinion, he would say to his companions:

"This is due to my sins."

He would repent to Allāh, and at times would stand in prayer until the matter became clear. He would then say: *"My hope is that I have been forgiven."* [28]

It is not hard to see why Imam Abū Ḥanīfah had the impact he did on not only his students, but also wider society. Every time Abū Ḥanīfah took a new student into his class, he would see to it that the student was properly clothed and had a

---

[27] Abu Bakr Ahmad bin Ali al-Khatīb al-Baghdādi
Tahqiq, *Tarīkh Baghdād,* Dār al-Kutub al-'Ilmīyah, Vol 16, p 359.
[28] Ibn Ḥajar al-Haythamī, *Al-Khayrāt al-Hisān Fi Manaqib al-Imam al-A'zam Abi Hanīfah al-Nu'mān Kitab,* Matba'at al-Sa'adah, 1900, p 54.

comfortable house to live in with their family. He was even known to help them with their personal matters like delivering marriage proposals on behalf of his students. Imam Abū Ḥanīfah was a man of the people and cared deeply for his neighbours and the residents of Kufa. One of his senior students, Imam Zufar, would say that Imam Abū Ḥanīfah would make everybody around him comfortable – it did not matter if the person was rich, poor, ignorant or scholarly. He said, *"I have never seen a man more willing to listen to people's concerns and advise them."* Imam Abū Ḥanīfah knew that serving Islam meant being in service to your community.

Around the world today, Imam Abū Ḥanīfah's school of thought is the most widely adopted and it has been this way for the last 13 centuries. Both the Abbasid and Ottoman dynasties chose this school of thought as the one they would rule with, and this helped spread his madhab throughout Iraq, Syria, Palestine, Lebanon, Egypt, Pakistan, Afghanistan, Bangladesh, India and even China. Today, over half of the Muslim world follows the *madhhab* of Imam Abū Ḥanīfah.

In chains

The torture and death of Imam Abū Ḥanīfah

Like many of Islam's scholars, the end of Imam Abū Ḥanīfah's life was spent in cruel prison conditions. Because his teachings and work had become so influential, those in power were hoping they could get him on their side and make sure he only gave Islamic opinions that agreed with their own motives and what the government wanted. It was impossible however, for Imam Abū Ḥanīfah to not act with honesty and independence, so he refused to accept the position of Judge *(Qāḍī)* in the court of the rulers. This refusal led to the imprisonment and torture of Imam Abū Ḥanīfah. He was given the ultimatum that he could either accept the position of Chief Judge or be subjected to another round of torture. Facing an impossible situation, Imam Abū Ḥanīfah left Kufa altogether and went to Makkah. His time in the region of Hijaz lasted 6-7 years and it was here that he came face to face with another great Imam – Imam Mālik.

Both of these two great men would engage in vigorous discussion with one another, comparing and contrasting their understanding. They debated with the utmost respect and love for one another. So much so, that when Imam Mālik's students asked him about Imam Abū Ḥanīfah, he said: *"Don't you know Imam Abū Ḥanīfah? If he had tried to convince me that this pillar was made of gold instead of stone, I would have to believe it!"*

In turn, Imam Abū Ḥanīfah would send his main student Imam Abū Yūsuf to study with Imam Mālik and Abū Yūsuf was able to incorporate Imam Mālik's methodology within the Ḥanafī *madhhab*. His other main student, Muḥammad al-Shaybānī, also studied with Imam Mālik for 3 years. Meeting and learning from Imam Mālik strengthened Abū Ḥanīfah's understanding and school of thought and brought huge benefit to his students too.

After this time in the Hijaz, when Imam Abū Ḥanīfah deemed it safe to return to Kufa, he went back to his hometown secure in the knowledge that the new governor would not force any scholars into positions of authority. This didn't last long however, as very soon a new leader named Abū Jaʿfar al-Manṣūr came to power and wanted to ensure all scholars were only teaching things the government approved of. Again, he forcefully offered Imam Abū Ḥanīfah the position of Chief Judge – insisting he take it or be tortured. True to his principles, Imam Abū Ḥanīfah declined again and Abū Jaʿfar ordered his imprisonment and 110 lashes. This sent shock waves throughout society and there was great horror that a man so great could be treated like this.

Reflecting on that time, Imam Abū Ḥanīfah said himself, *"The grief that I knew my mother was experiencing because of my trial was more painful than the lashes."* [29]

Approaching the fragile age of 70, Imam Abū Ḥanīfah – the son of a wealthy merchant – spent his final days enduring cruel conditions in captivity. Days and nights passed with his body growing weaker and limbs struggling to find strength. Despite his physical weakness, the heart and mind of Imam Abū Ḥanīfah remained stronger than ever, as did his faith in Allāh.

While still shackled in heavy chains, in the year 150 AH, Imam Abū Ḥanīfah's soul left his body and returned to the Creator he spent his entire life serving. In one narration, Imam Abū Ḥanīfah passed away while in the state of sujūd. Some speculated that the Caliph at the time – al-Manṣūr – ordered for the food of Imam Abū Ḥanīfah to be poisoned. Only Allāh knows what the true reasons behind his devastating end were.

The outpouring of grief and distress at the loss of such a unique and unparalleled human being spread far and wide. Ibn Kathīr said: *"The funeral prayer of Imam Abū Ḥanīfah was conducted six times in Baghdad due to the vast numbers of people. His grave is there. May Allāh have mercy on him."* [30]

Al-Dhahabī wrote one volume on the life of each of the other three great Imams and said: *"The account of Abū Ḥanīfah's life requires two volumes."* When Imam Abū Ḥanīfah's son Ḥammād washed his father's body for burial, he said to him: *"May Allāh have mercy on you! You have exhausted whoever tries* to *catch*

[29] Abu Bakr Ahmad bin Ali al-Khatīb al-Baghdādi
Tahqiq, *Tarīkh Baghdād,* Dār al-Kutub al-'Ilmīyah, Vol 15, p 444.
[30] Ibn Katheer, *Al-Bidāya wa'l-Nihāyah,* Darrusalam Publications, Vol 10, p 115.

up with you." Such was the legacy of this incredible human being.

The mercy of Allāh is greater than any human mind can perceive and after losing one of the shining stars of our Ummah, that same year, another Imam would be born: Muḥammad ibn Idrīs al-Shāfiʿī.

This turn of events caused the scholars to reflect, *"A moon had died, and another was born."*

Lessons we can learn

Consider the sincerity of Thābit and what it got him

As a young man who let his yearning for a piece of fruit overcome him, Thābit felt a very sincere and deep regret for his actions. He went to great lengths to try to correct his wrong and when he was told something that would shock most people, his sincerity to Allāh won through. When we fall short in our own lives, we may not have to hypothetically accept a marriage offer to make up for it, but we should have the same commitment Thābit had to make things right again.

We will all make mistakes – major and minor ones – however, the door to Allāh's mercy is forever wide open. Do not ever think you have done anything that is beyond Allāh's capacity to forgive. The sincerity that Thābit had over a piece of fruit was rewarded in unimaginable ways – he married the mother of one of the greatest men who ever lived and had a son who will be a source of great joy in the Hereafter. Our sincerity – even after we make mistakes – can earn us rewards just as great and beautiful too.

Having money is a responsibility and a privilege

Imam Abū Ḥanīfah grew up with a father running an extremely successful business and inherited a handsome amount of wealth. This amount of money would have been enough for him to never need to work again. However, not only did he work, but he expanded his father's business and then – after his own needs were met – used all the extra wealth to serve those in need.

Imam Abū Ḥanīfah also used his money to sponsor students and through this, made a long-term investment. The good deeds we do may not necessarily pay off here and now, but sometimes you have to just sow the seeds. The young students that Imam Abū Ḥanīfah supported may have taken decades to become established scholars, but that doesn't matter – the real reward and payoff for those deeds will be in the Hereafter anyway. Think big and plan long term, not all rewards are immediate, in fact, some of the best ones aren't!

Imam Abū Ḥanīfah understood that having money puts you in a position of responsibility as Allāh will question us all about what we did to benefit others with it. He also understood that it is better to be the 'upper hand' (the one that gives) than be the 'lower hand' (the one that receives)[31] – so when we can give charity, we should be grateful we are in a position to give in the first place.

Don't underestimate the impact of a few words

A passing comment can be few in words, but extremely heavy in impact. In fact, a simple statement could be somebody's turning point in life. Imam Abū Ḥanīfah's turning point was being asked why his intelligence wasn't being used by visiting and learning from scholars, and this was enough for something inside him to switch. Often it is not the big and grand statements that make a difference, but a realisation or shift in perspective that can be triggered by a 'small' or 'unimportant' interaction – so keep your eyes and ears switched on! This was not an accident or coincidence, but all part of a grand plan set in motion by Allāh.

There is great power in the words we speak, both to motivate and inspire others as well as to impact and realise things ourselves.

---

[31] Imam Abul-Husain Muslim, *Ṣaḥiḥ Muslim*, Dar-us-Salam Publications Inc, 2007, P 1036.

How simple words led to huge transformations

- Shaykh al-Birzalī one day said to Imam al-Dhahabī: *"Your handwriting resembles the handwriting of the scholars of hadith."* Imam al-Dhahabī said, *"From that day onwards, Allāh placed the love of hadith within my heart."*

- Imam al-Bukhārī said he was once seated with Isḥāq ibn Rahawayh who casually asked, *"Why don't you gather a summarised book of the authentic narrations of the Prophet ﷺ?"* He says, *"Instantly the love of doing so fell into my heart and I began to compile the book."*

- Imam Bukhārī was only 16 years old at the time of hearing this and dedicated the next 16 years of his life to compile his book. This means he was only 32 years old when he completed his monumental project *(Ṣaḥīḥ al-Bukhārī)* which is today considered the most authentic book after the Qur'an.

- The great scholar Badr al-Dīn ibn Jamāʿah understood the importance of encouraging potential and said: *"Whenever we saw a young one exhibiting signs of intelligence, we would cast our nets over them, and they would only leave our tutelage after they had become a scholar."*

Siyar Aʿlām al-Nubalā'

Don't ever feel limited by your age

Imam Abū Ḥanīfah, and many scholars from the past, achieved many great things despite their youth. At only 20 years of age, Imam Abū Ḥanīfah had his genius recognised widely and never allowed others to limit his passions. Sometimes people might feel too old to accomplish a goal they consider very basic, and others might think they are too young to begin something monumental: both attitudes are wrong. The only limit is in your mind and the number of years you have lived so far should have no impact on your potential.

Do not be afraid to pursue your passion

Though Imam Abū Ḥanīfah had built a strong reputation for having a formidable talent in *Kalām* (and even travelled extensively to further strengthen his expertise), when the time came, he completely abandoned that area of study and pursued a different area of knowledge: *Fiqh.* Pursuing your passions might not always be as easy as picking up your shoes and joining another study circle, but it will be worth it. Allāh has placed special skills and unique talents within you, and it is your responsibility (and privilege) to unearth this and use it to benefit yourself and others. We all have a calling, be brave enough to find yours.

Learn from the best people available to you

When Imam Abū Ḥanīfah found his teacher Ḥammād, he knew that he was not going to find anybody else who could teach him what Ḥammād could. Thus, he stayed by his side and gained as much benefit as he could from his teacher. For all subjects we study (and especially matters of religion), we should seek out the best, most qualified people to teach us. We are going to be absorbing the ideas and knowledge of our teachers as they present it, so it is extremely important the people who teach us have earned the right to do just that. Knowledge is powerful and should be treated with care and caution.

Things will come to you at the right time

When Imam Abū Ḥanīfah felt an inkling in his heart to separate away from his teacher and start up his own independent study circle, Allāh taught him that it was not the right time. Ḥammād's absence meant that Imam Abū Ḥanīfah had to take on his role and during this time, he realised he was not as qualified in the role as he originally thought. Eventually, when the time was right, he fulfilled this very same role with excellence.

We might want something here and now, but it might not be the best time to receive it. We might have to go through some learning and growth first in order to achieve it. Holding back and being patient means that what you want will come to you in the best way – with Allāh's perfect timing and according to His perfect wisdom. It might be a bitter and impatient wait, but only in hindsight will you see that everything worked out exactly as it was meant to for your benefit.

The purpose of knowledge is action and growth

Imam Abū Ḥanīfah was an intellectual powerhouse. He was a skilled debater, memoriser, academic and scholar. However, all the knowledge wasn't just neatly stored in his head and rolled out for his students during lessons. He increased in his outward worship every time he came across new knowledge and never neglected putting things into practice.

He understood that the purpose of knowledge is for you to increase in benefit, good actions, personal growth and impact. If you are learning more things about Islam but are not becoming a better person to yourself and those around you, then something hasn't fully clicked yet. We are not people who worship as a set of robotic rituals, but those whose worship makes them better in their character and dealings with people. Don't stagnate with abstract knowledge alone, put it into practice with concrete action.

The benefits of collaboration

The entire process of coming up with rulings within Imam Abū Ḥanīfah's school of thought relied on collaboration, discussion and pooling together the best skills and talents of the people within his circle. There is strength in listening to and considering different perspectives as, together, these build a broader and more complete perspective on any given issue.

You do not have to be trying to come up with an Islamic legal ruling to see the huge benefit of collaborating with others. Each of us has important insights that others may not have and likewise, we are always able to learn things from the knowledge and experience of others. The richest understanding of life will come from considering multiple perspectives and having the humility to listen and accept that everybody can benefit us in some way.

Never write people off as a lost cause

When Imam Abū Ḥanīfah's drunken neighbour would wail and warble all night long, it would have been all too easy to look down on this man and think no good could come of him. Imam Abū Ḥanīfah, however, showed concern and a sincere regard for his neighbour's welfare. He looked deeper than the surface portrayal of 'a loud, drunk neighbour' and saw him for the person he was, and the potential he had for reformation.

He also used his privilege as a respected scholar to help the marginalised and despised of society, showing compassion towards them over arrogance or judgement. In his duty to help his neighbour, he opened up the opportunity for this drunken neighbour to repent and transform his life. The attitude of mercy and softness towards others has the incredible potential to change the course of someone's life, especially those who you think least 'deserve' it. Listen and accept that everybody can benefit us in some way.

Imam Mālik

1

Full name: Mālik son of Anas son of Mālik son of Abī ʿĀmir son of ʿAmr son of Al-Ḥārith son of Ghaymān son of Khuthayl son of ʿAmr son of Al-Ḥārith al-Aṣbaḥī al-Ḥumyarī al-Madanī

Born in: Madinah 93 AH/711 CE

Died in: Madinah - 179 AH/795 CE (lived for 84 years)

Best known works: *Al-Muwaṭṭa', Al-Mudawwanah*

Out playing with birds...

In the year 2 AH, the Yemeni Abū ʿAmir decided to leave his old life behind and embrace the new religion he had learned about called Islam. He migrated from Yemen to Madinah and alongside the Prophet Muḥammad ﷺ participated in most of the battles that the Muslims fought. Abū ʿAmir was brave, faithful and had high aspirations for his progeny to come.

Just 90 years later, the great-grandson of Abū ʿAmir would be born in Madinah – a fair-haired, green-eyed boy named Mālik ibn Anas.

One day the young Mālik was play fighting with his older brother when their father gestured for them to come over. Still panting, both boys sat on either side of their father as he tested them both with an Islamic question. Quick to answer, Mālik's brother got the answer right while Mālik himself was still figuring out the question.

Mālik was different from his brother in many ways – he looked different and now it seemed he wasn't as quick at answering questions too.

Looking down at his younger son, Mālik's father ruffled his hair and said smiling, *"I think playing with birds has distracted you from the quest for knowledge, my boy."* [32]

It was true, young Mālik did love to spend hours playing with the birds of Madinah. However, not being able to answer his father's question and seeing his brother look so pleased with himself caused Mālik to declare, *"Right, that's it! I'm going to find Ibn Hurmuz!"* Ibn Hurmuz was the nickname for the local scholar ʿAbdullāh ibn Yazīd, who was from the *Tābiʿīn.* **(See: What are the Tābiʿ īn?)** He was one of the best scholars of the area and Mālik was determined to become his student.

Full of enthusiasm, young Mālik now made it a habit to wake up extra early (and definitely earlier than his

---

[32] Burhan al Din Abu al-Wafa' Ibrahim Ibn Farhun, *Al-Dibaj al-Mudhahhab fī Ma'rifat A'yān 'Ulamā' al-Madhhab*, Turath For Solutions, 2013, Vol 1, p 99.

brother!) and learn from Ibn Hurmuz, not leaving him until late into the night. This continued for 7 years, much to the delight of his parents. Imam Mālik recalls how his mother encouraged his learning and made clear what his priorities should be: *"My mother would tie a turban around my head and say, 'Go to study - but learn from your teacher's manners before you learn from his knowledge!'"* [33]

She believed that the foundation for all good action could only come from having good character first.

Manners first, knowledge next...

The theme of perfecting manners before beginning formal learning is something that was understood by Islamic scholars. After all, what use is your learning if you put people off you because of bad character, poor manners and impatience?

- Sufyān al-Thawrī said: *"Students of knowledge would only embark on their journey for knowledge when they had first acquired manners and exerted huge efforts in worship for 20 years."* (Ḥilyat al-Awliyā')

- Makhlad ibn al-Ḥusayn said: *"We are in need of a few good manners than huge amounts of knowledge."* (Madārij al-Sālikīn)

- The Companions would say to their children: *"My child, for you to master a chapter on manners is dearer to me than for you to master seventy chapters of knowledge." (Tadhkirat al-Sāmiʿ wa al-Mutakallim fī Adab al-ʿĀlim wa al-Mutaʿallim)*

---

[33] Burhan al-Din Abu al-Wafa' Ibrahim Ibn Farhun, *Al-Dībāj al-Mudhahhab fī Ma'rifat A'yān 'Ulamā' al-Madhhab,* Turath For Solutions, 2013, Vol 1, p 99.

Experiencing many different teachers and students

As Mālik grew, he went on to study under Nāfiʿ, who was the freed slave of Ibn ʿUmar – who himself was a servant of the Prophet ﷺ. This connection made a very short chain of students/teachers from Mālik to the Prophet ﷺ and is known as "Silsilat al-dhahab" i.e. the Golden Chain.

Another one of his teachers was a scholar named Ibn Shihāb, a man who was always very busy and had little spare time for students outside of class. Imam Mālik recalls one of his encounters with Ibn Shihāb:

"On one Eid day I said to myself, *'This is surely a day when Ibn Shihāb will have a bit more time.'* So after prayer, I sat at his door. I heard him say to his servant, *'Go and see who is at the door.'* I heard the servant say, *'It is your fair-haired student, Mālik.'* Ibn Shihāb said, *'Allow him in.'*

Once I entered, he said to me, *'Have you not gone home?'* I said *'No.'*

He said, *'Have you eaten anything?'* I said *'No.'*

He said, *'What do you want?'* I said, *'For you to relate hadith to me.'*

So Ibn Shihāb narrated seventeen hadith to me and after he finished, he leant in and asked quizzically, *'What use is this knowledge, if you do not memorise it?'*

I said, *'I can repeat every one of them to you,'* and I did just that. Stunned by what he had just witnessed, Ibn Shihāb leant back and said in adoration, *'What an excellent vessel of knowledge you are.'*" [34]

Once Imam Mālik had spent years learning under many different teachers, he began to teach students himself. One of his most famous students (and another one of our Four Imams) was Imam al-Shāfiʿī who memorised Imam Mālik's main book *al-Muwaṭṭa'* when he was only 17 years old. The *Muwaṭṭa'* is a book of *hadith* and *fiqh* that includes over 1720 narrations from the Prophet ﷺ, Companions, and the Tābiʿīn.

As Imam Mālik was stationed in Madinah, many of his students took on the role of travelling to different regions to teach from the works of their teacher. One particular student, ʿAbd al-Raḥmān ibn Qāsim al-Miṣrī, played a strong role in spreading the Mālikī school of thought as far as Morocco, Egypt, Sudan and al-Andalus. Students from these regions would travel to meet and learn from ʿAbd al-Raḥmān ibn Qāsim and then would go back to spread his teachings among their own communities. Along with ʿAbd al-Raḥmān ibn Qāsim, two other students of Imam Mālik – Asad ibn al-Furāt and Saḥnūn – came together to

---

[34] Al-Qaadi 'Iyaad, *Tartīb al-Madārik wa Taqrīb al-Masalik,* Dār al-Kutub al-'Ilmīyah, Beirut 1997, Vol 1, p 130.

author *al-Mudawwanah*, the core text in the Mālikī school of thought.

Often, observing a teacher's students can tell you a lot about the person they have learnt from. Imam Mālik didn't just teach people his knowledge, he created a movement within many generations of students to pass on the precious knowledge far and wide. Al-Fuḍayl ibn ʿIyāḍ names over 1300 students of Imam Mālik who studied directly with him, but in reality, the true number would simply be far too many to count.

Imam Mālik himself understood what kinds of sacrifices he had to make to access the best of teachers and was willing to pay the price. Not a rich man by background, Ibn Qāsim said of him:

"Mālik's quest and expenditure for seeking knowledge resulted in him needing to sell the roof of his house for the price of its wood. Later on in life, the world opened up for him." [35]

Imam Mālik's teachers were the most well-known jurists of Madinah, and from the Tābiʿīn themselves. This was a special privilege given to Imam Mālik as he was in what would be considered the heartland of Islamic knowledge – the city of the Prophet ﷺ – al-Madinah.

Knowing the culture of scholarship that he was blessed to be part of, Imam Mālik said about himself: *"I have assumed the position of being able to give an Islamic ruling only after seventy scholars have testified that I am fit to do so."* [36]

This shows the heavy weight of responsibility that rests on the shoulders of the one who issues rulings within Islam – it is considered a great trust and never taken lightly. Scholars would be cautious and hesitate to make claims about any areas of knowledge unless they felt fully confident in the absolute strength of their position.

---

[35] Al-Qaadi 'Iyaad, Tartīb al-Madārik wa Taqrīb al-Masalik, Dār al-Kutub al-'Ilmīyah, Beirut 1997, Vol 1, p 130.
[36] Al-Qaadi 'Iyaad, Tartīb al-Madārik wa Taqrīb al-Masalik, Dār al-Kutub al-'Ilmīyah, Beirut, 1997, Vol 1, p 142.

The character of Imam Mālik

His caution against seeking fame

Everything in life happens according to the careful Plan of Allāh, and the greatest testimony for Imam Mālik's status may well have been from a prediction of the Prophet Muḥammad ﷺ:

"It shall soon be that people will be hastening on camelback seeking knowledge, but they will not find anyone more knowledgeable than the scholar of Madinah." [37]

Because he was not named explicitly, we cannot guarantee it was Imam Mālik being spoken of here. However, several great scholars – including Sufyān ibn ʿUyaynah and ʿAbd al-Razzāq – have stated that the scholar mentioned, is in reference to Imam Mālik.

Just like Imam Abū Ḥanīfah before him, and Imam al-Shāfiʿī and Imam Aḥmad after him, Imam Mālik was extremely cautious about his growing popularity and fame. He understood the risk of his intentions becoming corrupted if he started to believe the hype others were creating and preferred to live privately and out of the public eye as much as possible.

In fact, he was often known to say: "*Whoever aspires for an opening of goodness to be made in his heart, to be saved from the throes of death and grief on the Day of Judgment, let him ensure that more of his good deeds are in private as opposed to public.*" [38]

Imam Mālik knew that as soon as somebody begins to show off their deeds in public, they run a very great risk of seeking the pleasure of the people, rather than the pleasure of Allāh. Everybody has an ego and without disciplining it, we can easily fall into the trap of pride and self-admiration. This contaminates the intention behind our worship and deeds and means that despite outwardly

[37] Muhammad ibn Isa ibn Surah al-Tirmidhī, Jami al-Tirmidhī, Darrusalam Publications 2007, Vol 4, p 344.

[38] Al-Qaadi 'Iyaad, Tartīb al-Madārik wa *Taqrīb al-Masalik,* Dār al-Kutub al-'Ilmīyah, Beirut, 1997, Vol 2, p 51.

being seen as righteous our inward state might be falling well short. It is better to focus all our energy on doing our deeds in a way that protects them from other people's eyes and keeping our actions special by preserving them only for Allāh's Knowledge.

Imam Mālik said: *"I have not acquired this knowledge for anyone but myself. I did not acquire it so that people need me, and this was the same attitude as the scholars of the past."*

His gravity of presence

Some people in life have a certain gravitas to their presence, so much so that, without saying a word, they can evoke awe from those around them. Imam Mālik was one such figure. He was seen as somebody whose dignity and dedication to knowledge was so strong, that those around him would immediately be cautious and guarded about their behaviour in his presence.

Saʿīd b. Abī Maryam said: *"I have never seen anyone of greater awe than Mālik. In fact, his prestige surpassed that of the Sultan."* [39]

The study circles of Imam Mālik did not have lots of conversation, discussion and back-and-forth between teacher and students. Instead, they were characterised by a serenity and seriousness as students maintained utmost focus on the teaching.

Ibn Qaʿnab said: *"I have never seen a gathering that had greater reverence than the assembly of Mālik. It was as if birds were sat on their heads."* [40]

Imam Mālik himself treated every class as a special event that deserved preparation and the best of etiquettes. Before class, he would bathe, wear his finest clothes, perfume himself and have scented incense lit for the purpose of honouring the knowledge he was about to teach.

Imagine then, being a student who walks into this well-prepared environment. It was an unspoken mental signal that something of great importance was about to take place. Filling the class with fine fragrance and perfect lighting made the students associate the serene teachings they were about to sit through with the beautiful environment around them.

In these study circles, Imam Mālik's students would slowly turn the pages of their book and quietly sharpen their pencils, being as discreet as possible. Even the leading scholars who would sit in his gatherings would never interrupt him

[39] Al-Qaadi *'Iyaad, Tartīb al-Madārik wa Taqrīb al-Masalik*, Dār al-Kutub al-'Ilmīyah, Beirut, 1997, Vol 2, p 33.
[40] Al-Qaadi *'Iyaad, Tartīb al-Madārik wa Taqrīb al-Masalik*, Dār al-Kutub al-'Ilmīyah, Beirut, 1997, Vol 2, p 33.

as he was teaching, and everyone had their eyes lowered in respect when the class started.

Not all the circles of scholars were like this. Every scholar had a particular way and enforced etiquettes that were important to them. This was the way Imam Mālik wanted to teach his students about the manners and high esteem that should be given to Islamic knowledge.

His unbreakable focus while teaching

As such a stoic and serious character, Imam Mālik would not let anything distract him from what he was teaching. Out in Madinah, this sometimes led to memorable incidents. One of his students Yaḥyā ibn Yaḥyā al-Andalusī recalls: *"I was sat with Mālik when two geckos landed on his head. They walked on Mālik's hat then made their way to his neck, until they were beneath his clothes and left from the bottom of his garment, while Mālik remained unfazed and unmoved."*

This was further followed by a shocking occurrence narrated by ʿAbdullāh ibn al-Mubārak who witnessed the following:

"I was with Mālik while he was conveying hadith when a scorpion stung him sixteen times. Mālik's colour began to change as he told himself not to interrupt the hadith of the Prophet ﷺ he was narrating. When the study circle ended and people dispersed, I said to him: 'Father of ʿAbdullāh! I saw something in you that baffled me!' Mālik said: *'Yes, I showed patience in order to honour the hadith of the Prophet ﷺ.'"* [41] It is worth noting here that Imam Mālik reacted this way because of his own personal dedication to his teaching, and this doesn't mean that we should allow ourselves (or others) to come to harm. The teachings of our Prophet ﷺ always taught us to look after our physical and mental wellbeing.

[41] Al-Qaadi 'Iyaad, *Tartīb al-Madārik wa Taqrīb al-Masalik*, Dār al-Kutub al-'Ilmīyah, Beirut, 1997, Vol 2, p 15.

His willingness to say "I don't know"

We live in a time where most people eagerly share their opinions and commentaries on a wide range of topics, to anybody who is willing to listen. Despite being an unparalleled vessel of knowledge, Imam Mālik would rarely make confident statements on Islamic matters unless he was absolutely certain beyond doubt that he was correct. It was not rare for him to say, "I don't know" in response to questions and felt no shame or embarrassment in doing so.

His student Ibn Wahb said: *"If I was so inclined, I could fill my scrolls documenting the sheer number of times Mālik said, 'I don't know.'"* [42]

In fact, a man once asked Imam Mālik forty-eight questions, and for thirty-two of them, Imam Mālik said "I don't know." [43]

Understanding the limits of knowledge and having the humility to say "I don't know" on topics you are not certain of is a rare and precious quality. Sometimes, people may be inclined to make up answers because they feel embarrassed or because they don't want to be judged or seen by others as not smart enough. This was not the attitude of the Prophet Muhammad ﷺ or the great scholars of our tradition.

The Prophet ﷺ once said: *"I do not know if the people of Tubba' were cursed or not. I do not know if Dhū'l-Qarnayn was a prophet or not. I do not know if capital punishment cleanses a person from sins or not."* [44]

This approach was not uncommon amongst even the nearest of the Companions of the Prophet ﷺ, as Ibn Mas'ūd said: *"Whoever provides an answer to every question that is posed to him is insane."* [45]

When the Companions of the Prophet ﷺ were confronted with a question, rather than rushing to be the one to answer and showing off their knowledge, they in fact, did the opposite.

'Abd al-Raḥmān ibn Abī Laylā said:

"I met 120 Companions of the Prophet ﷺ. One of them would be asked a question, so he would refer him to someone else, and that someone would refer him to someone else, until the question would return back to the first person. Each and every one of them wished that his brother would spare him the burden of answering."

Once a student of Imam Mālik asked him a question to which he replied, "I

[42] Ibn 'Abd al-Bar, *Jāmi' Bayān al-'Ilm wa Fadlih,* Darul Imam Bukhari, Vol 2, p 838.
[43] Ibn 'Abd al-Barr, *Al-Intiqā' fī Faḍā'il al-Thalāthat al-A'immah al-Fuqahā'*, Dar al-Islam al-Bashayr al-Islamiyyah, Vol 1, p 38.
[44] Al-Bayhaqi, *Mustadrak al-Hakim,* Vol 1, p 92.
[45] Ibn 'Abd al-Barr, *Jāmi' Bayān al-'Ilm wa Fadlih,* Darul Imam Bukhari, Vol 2, p 1124.

don't know." Unsatisfied, the student casually pressed his teacher further saying, *"Come on, it is only a light matter."* This infuriated Imam Mālik who said: *"No aspect of knowledge is light! Have you not read the verse where Allāh said, 'We shall send down to you a heavy word'?"* [46]

This was the approach and way of all the great Imams. We will return to the concept of "I don't know" when exploring the life of Imam Aḥmad.

His preference for simplicity

Despite Imam Mālik's immense popularity amongst the people, he did not grow in material wealth or have any riches. In fact, he did not even own a house. Imam Mālik himself was a tenant in a house that belonged to the great Companion ʿAbdullāh ibn Masʿūd. One thing that was important to Imam Mālik, however, was presenting himself in fine clothing. He believed as a teacher, he was a representative of sacred knowledge delivering a message that should be given in the best of ways. Presenting himself in impeccable clothing was, therefore, part of his worship and commitment to beautifying knowledge - not merely for vanity or trying to impress others.

[46] Qur'an 73: 5.

His indifference towards power and privilege

Imam Mālik was a fiercely principled man and refused to have his opinions influenced by those around him who held power and status. He had in fact once issued a religious ruling *(fatwā)* that went against the ruling Caliph Hārūn al-Rashīd wanted and was severely punished for it.

Despite this, the Caliph came to Madinah and asked Imam Mālik to teach hadith to his princes at the palace. Unmoved by this offer, Imam Mālik replied, *"The wealth of knowledge does not go to the door of others"*, meaning that the princes would not get special treatment and would be treated just like the rest of his other students.

Relenting, Hārūn al-Rashīd then came himself with his princes and attended the study circle of Imam Mālik like everybody else. This was a lesson in humility for the Caliph as he learnt that if you want to access Islamic learning, then you must first humble yourself and come to where the lessons are taking place. Even as a Caliph, do not expect knowledge to travel to you.

A letter from 'Abdullāh

The scholar ʿAbdullāh ibn ʿAbd al-ʿAzīz al-ʿUmarī once wrote a letter to Imam Mālik encouraging him to distance himself from public gatherings and to free up his time for seclusion and worship. After reading and carefully considering the contents of the letter, Imam Mālik penned his response: [47]

Dear ʿAbdullāh,

Allāh has spread good deeds amongst people the same way He has spread their provisions of money, health and family. One person's heart might be open towards prayer but might not be open towards fasting. Another person's heart might be inclined towards charity, but not feel the same way towards fasting. Another person might be eager for jihad, but not so keen on performing extra prayers.
The way I teach knowledge is one of the most rewarding good deeds, and I am happy and grateful that Allāh has opened this up for me.
I do not believe what I am busy doing is anything less than what you are busy doing. My hope is that we are both upon goodness and each of us should be grateful for the things that Allāh has made possible for us.

Salām,

Mālik

Hanging up al-Muwatta' in the Ka'bah

As Imam Mālik's teachings spread and his popularity grew, those in power began to pay close attention to this scholar and what he had to say. The Abbasid Caliph at the time – Abū Jaʿfar al-Manṣūr – was so taken by Imam Mālik and his knowledge that he wanted to hang a copy of his famous book,

[47] Ibn 'Abd al-Barr, *Al-Tamhīd*, Vol 7, p 185.

al-Muwaṭṭa', up in the Ka'bah. The *Muwaṭṭa'* was the crowning glory of Imam Mālik's scholarly achievements and is still studied around the world today. Imam Mālik compiled the *Muwaṭṭa'* after examining hundreds of thousands of hadiths, then hand-picking a smaller number of the most authentic ones and organising them by subject like Prayer, *Zakat* and Fasting.

Caliph al-Manṣūr wanted to take the *Muwaṭṭa'* and impose the rulings within the book on the entire Caliphate (Muslim lands under his control). He was ready to instruct all the scholars to only issue rulings according to what was in the *Muwaṭṭa'.*

An opportunity like this was something that most people could only dream of. Not only to have your work given the highest honour by being held in the place that all Muslims turn for prayer, but also having your teachings made the standard that the rest of the Muslim world must follow.

Despite so much opportunity, brought right to his door, Imam Mālik was sure of what he wanted to do. He respectfully declined Caliph al-Manṣūr's offer and strongly advised him not to go through with this plan. The lure of fame didn't interest Imam Mālik in the slightest.

He told the Caliph that different Companions of the Prophet ﷺ had spread throughout the land, conveying different parts of the tradition that others may not have had access to, so imposing one interpretation on the entire Muslim community would be unfair. He would say, *"Refrain from this as the Companions of the Prophet ﷺ themselves held opposing views on subsidiary matters."* In a time where he could have cemented world-wide recognition for himself and his work, Imam Mālik chose the path of sincerity, remaining true to the way of the Prophet ﷺ and his blessed Companions.

Al-Muwaṭṭa': Quick facts

- *'Al-Muwaṭṭa'* means "The Well-Trodden" because it is a text that made knowledge accessible and easy (waṭṭa'a) for the people.
- The book was approved by 70 scholars.
- It contains 1720 hadith.
- Imam Mālik compiled *al-Muwaṭṭa'* over the course of 40 years.
- *Al-Muwaṭṭa'* originally began as 10,000 narrations that were then whittled down to their current number.
- Imam Bukhārī said that the most authentic chain of transmission is called "Silsilat al-Dhahab" (The Golden Chain) which has only 3 links: The **Prophet** ﷺ to **ʿIbn Umar** to **Nāfiʿ** to **Mālik.**
- There are 80 narrations with the Golden Chain in *al-Muwaṭṭa'.*

The children of Imam Mālik

It is easy to assume that when you have a father like Imam Mālik, the path to scholarship would be the natural route. But just like many of our Imams didn't come from a line of scholars, many of them also didn't leave behind scholars either. Imam Mālik had four children, most of them showed little interest in their father's knowledge or activities. When any of them did attend his study circles - like his sons Yaḥyā and Muḥammad sometimes would - it would be short lived, dipping in and out. The world may have held Imam Mālik in great esteem and treated him with the utmost awe and respect, however his children were a different story.

Imam Mālik would say: *"Remembering that this knowledge cannot be passed down like an inheritance is what brings me solace."* [48]

[48] Al-Qaadi 'Iyaad, *Tartīb al-Madārik wa Taqrīb al-Masalik*, Dār al-Kutub al-'Ilmīyah, Beirut, 1997, Vol 1, p 117.

What he meant by this is that he would avoid feeling so disheartened about his children's lack of interest in Islamic knowledge, because he knew that ultimately this is a gift given by Allāh and not simply something handed down from one generation to the next, like an heirloom.

Another fact about Imam Mālik's children is that it was only his daughter Fātima that took a strong interest in her father's scholarship and became a scholar herself. Unlike her brothers, she had memorised the Muwaṭṭa' and was eager to absorb what her father was teaching to his students. During his classes, she would stand on the other side of the door - distancing herself from the gathering of men - and would listen to the readings taking place. If any of the men made a mistake, she would gently knock on the door, and this would alert her father to correct it.

In our history there have been families - and entire dynasties - made up of scholars who passed on the thirst for learning from one generation to the next. Likewise, there have also been many instances of families who didn't have a background in Islamic learning but raised children who became the greatest scholars of all times. Like many of our Prophets, scholars too had children who didn't listen to them, follow in their footsteps, or secure a legacy for themselves. It is a comfort to the heart - and a reminder to stay humble - to understand that the desire for Islamic learning is something Allāh blesses people with and not, as we can see, an automatic right you have because of who or what your parents are.

Being tested by a secret spy

Like the other great Imams spoken of here, Imam Mālik had a difficult relationship with the ruling powers of his time. Though he was never put to torture or imprisoned like the others, Imam Mālik struggled against the state officials in Madinah. Anybody who seemed to have people loyal to them caused concern for those in power.

With the passing of time, Imam Mālik became the most famous scholar of all time. Unlike the other three great Imams, whose popularity grew more after their death, Imam Mālik's popularity reached its peak during his lifetime, and the authorities had a keen eye on him as a result.

Caliph Manṣūr was particularly interested in Imam Mālik and his opinions, and watched as a trick question was one day presented to the Imam: *"If a man was forced to divorce his wife, would the divorce still count?"*

Imam Mālik replied: *"The divorce of the one who is forced does not take effect."*

The ruling authorities did not like this answer. At the time, they were forcing people to support the Caliph by pledging allegiance to him though they did not want to. They were worried that if people heard you cannot force someone to divorce their spouse, then they would believe you cannot force someone to support a Caliph they didn't like.

After the Imam was asked this once, a spy was sent from the Caliph to ask him the same question again. Imam Mālik gave the same answer a second time. The governor of Madinah (who happened to be the cousin of the Caliph) was waiting outside and immediately entered when he heard the answer again. He seized Imam Mālik and took him away to be lashed. Imam Mālik was assaulted so viciously that both of his arms were dislocated, and he fell unconscious from the beating. Upon rousing and with his body bloodied and bruised, Imam Mālik opened his mouth as the guards leaned in to hear what his first words would be. *"The divorce of the coerced is null and void,"* Imam Mālik spoke out, despite the severe pain in his body. His stance was not going to shift. Unsure what to do, the guards reported Imam Mālik's statement to their seniors who then relayed it back to Caliph Manṣūr. Exasperated and knowing he was fighting a losing battle, Caliph Manṣūr ordered the release of Imam Mālik and decided to keep a close eye on him instead.

The death of a giant

Imam Mālik spent his entire life in Madinah, only leaving once for hajj, where he would meet Imam Abū Ḥanīfah. Several Caliphs of his time tried to persuade him to move to Baghdad, however Imam Mālik preferred Madinah over all other cities.

At the age of 84, Imam Mālik fell ill, and his health continued to decline. On the 14th of Rabīʿ al-Awwal 179 AH (795 CE), Imam Mālik passed away in his beloved city of Madinah. The news of his death engulfed the entire Ummah with grief, and many remarked that a man like Imam Mālik could never be found on the face of this earth again. The Amīr of Madinah, ʿAbd al-ʿAzīz ibn Muhammad, led his funeral prayers and he was laid to rest in the distinguished graveyard of al-Baqīʿ.

Following his death, Imam Mālik's school of thought would spread across almost the entire North African region – from Libya to Mauritania, including Sudan. There was also a time when the Mālikī school of thought was dominant in Egypt, Basra (in Iraq), the Arabian Peninsula and other parts of the Islamic world. The life and legacy of Imam Mālik has, therefore, been immortalised for all of time.

Lessons we can learn

Knowledge without manners is futile

As Imam Mālik's mother lovingly prepared her young son for his lessons – wrapping his turban with care – she understood that the path to learning could only be built on good manners. She made sure to stress to her son that having a lot of knowledge in your head was separate from having good character – and one was useless without the other. This is why many scholars of the past focused on learning manners, appropriate etiquettes and the correct state of heart one should have, before opening a book and memorising narrations.

Imagine you have a teacher who knows a great deal about the subject they teach. They might even be experts in their field. Now imagine they have a harsh, arrogant or impatient manner to them. Would their knowledge ever benefit their students? Would people want to even be around them long enough to learn from them?

Without good manners, you cannot benefit others with your knowledge – and you are likely not benefitting yourself either. Imam Mālik's mother understood this keenly, and she therefore prioritised the teaching of manners before the learning of knowledge. When he grew up, Imam Mālik realised that as a teacher, he represented the knowledge itself. So not only did he take his responsibility seriously, but he wore his best clothes to his lessons and lit beautiful fragrances for his students too. Beautiful knowledge should be complemented by beautiful teaching manner and, where possible, beautiful settings and environments too.

Don't underestimate the power of memorisation

Today, memorising seems to be a lost art. Not so long ago, it used to be common to memorise poetry, great speeches, multiplication tables and even rules of grammar. This fell out of favour in recent times as technology advanced and many mistakenly came to believe it was unproductive.

Memorising is a workout for your brain. Memory not only lets you store and retrieve the information you learn, but that stored information in your memory provides you with a framework to link new knowledge by association. It is like laying out a neurological roadmap in your head that you can continue to add new junctions and roads to. Memorising therefore sharpens your brain and allows you to build a vast internal library that you can literally carry with you anywhere you go!

In our tradition, as Muslims, memorisation was considered the foundation to learning and, like in the case of Imam Mālik and his Muwaṭṭa' – was a prerequisite to learning in the first place. Once you have committed important information to memory, you can forever learn more about it and uncover deeper insights and richer meanings from it. At an older age, you might not have the memory power you do now, so take advantage of this gift of easy memorisation in your younger age. In a world where everything comes to us at a quick click or swipe, revisit the incredible power of memorisation for yourself and your learning journey.

Consider the chain reactions you could start off...

Imam Mālik was one man and had limited hours in the day and a limited life span too. Somehow, in that time, he managed to secure an eternal legacy for himself that was carried by his amazing students. The things that Imam Mālik taught his students wove themselves into a chain of knowledge that was passed down for countless generations and has impacted millions of people. We might not have the time to reach millions of people ourselves, but the beauty of a sincere intention is that we can carry on watching our good deeds multiply (long after our lifespans) as people pass on what they know to others, and they pass it on to others, and so on.

From the generosity of Allāh is that we will continue to reap the reward for beneficial deeds we put out there, while others still get their full reward too. *"Whoever guides someone to goodness will have a reward like one who did it."* [49]

Don't underestimate the power you have to impact others. Look at what Imam Mālik – a fellow human being like you – managed to achieve in his lifetime. What will your 'chain reaction' look like?

The beauty of keeping your good deeds private

In a world where it is easy to show off every aspect of our lives to family, friends and strangers, it is more important than ever to resist the urge to be seen, noticed and praised by others. One way to preserve the sincerity of our deeds is to do them in private and keep our efforts between ourselves and Allāh.

It is easy for us to fall into the trap of wanting to look good or be admired by others, however, true confidence comes from within. Wanting to impress others can have grave consequences on our deeds, when we perform them to boost our ego or show off. To preserve the sincerity of our deeds and keep our intentions purely for Allāh, try to begin a regular habit of picking a good deed and performing it in secret, away from the eyes and ears of others. Ask Allāh to protect you from wanting to be seen or admired by people and to keep your heart focused purely on attaining His Pleasure.

[49] Imam Abul-Husain Muslim, Ṣaḥīḥ Muslim, Dar-us-Salam Publications Inc, 2007, Vol 4, p 2060.

Private acts of worship you can do without anyone knowing

- Wake up before Fajr and pray 2 rakʿahs of ṣalāh as part of tahajjud.
- Separate out a certain amount of money every week to give in charity.
- Pick one of the special Sunnah times for fasting and try fasting it regularly.
- Take some time out in the day to sit alone and make long and focused duʿa for yourself, your family and the Ummah.
- Use the moments when you are waiting around for discreet adhkār (words of remembrance) throughout the day.

The power of "I don't know"

We live in a time where many people have strong opinions on a startling range of subjects. Not only do we think we know a lot, now we have access to platforms where we can instantaneously declare our expert analysis to audiences around the world. Nobody wants to feel judged or lesser in the eyes of others by having less knowledge, so a common trap is to fake expertise in topics just to be seen as intelligent and relevant. The irony of this, however, is that the people who are truly learned and regarded as 'experts' in their field are extremely cautious about the statements they put out, and hardly ever make simplistic and bold statements on topics.

It takes a great deal of humility and sincerity to simply say "I don't know" when you are unsure. In fact, saying "I don't know" is not a sign of ignorance, but rather a sign of strength, integrity and courage. It is also an invitation for further learning and enquiry.

The scholars of our tradition understood that the knowledge they were learning required an extra level of care and caution, as they were speaking about Allāh and His Prophet ﷺ. This made them extremely careful about the statements they made and the answers they gave when people would ask them questions. They understood it was very risky to get an answer wrong as this could harm people and their practice of Islam. Imam Mālik understood the weight of his responsibility and therefore frequently and comfortably replied "I don't know" to many questions.

Often it is a sign of deep knowledge to not give strong answers to complicated questions, but instead to acknowledge our current limits. It is always better to be careful when speaking on matters of religion as we are dealing with a believer's understanding of Islam, their choices in life and ultimately, the health of their soul. At all times, therefore, treat your words and statements with care and deep consideration.

Appreciate that everybody has their own path in life

When a well-meaning ʿAbdullāh ibn ʿAbd al-ʿAzīz wrote to Imam Mālik, he believed that it would be better for him to abandon teaching and take up other forms of worship. Understanding himself and the inclination he had, Imam Mālik replied with confidence that he felt grateful for the path he had been put on, and not everybody has to take the same direction to Allāh's pleasure.

In life, everybody will have ways of learning and acts of worship that are naturally easier for them than others. They may find a certain act of worship easy and enjoyable but struggle hugely with another. This is okay. We have all been created differently, with different talents, interests and abilities. What you enjoy is usually what you will become good at, and what your heart will incline to. You can pursue your path and ally yourself with others who focus on a different path to Allāh's pleasure – the path is wide and designed to accommodate all the types of good actions within it.

Turning down immense worldly rewards for a much greater pay out

Of all the humans to have ever existed, very few could ever be in the position where a book they had authored would be invited to hang in the Kaʿbah, by the most powerful leader of that time. Hanging up al-Muwaṭṭa' in the Kaʿbah – and imposing its rulings on the entire Muslim Caliphate – would have catapulted Imam Mālik's fame hugely. However, despite this, the idea immediately did not sit well with Imam Mālik and went directly against his convictions, as well as his intellectual honesty. He turned down an offer that would have propelled his status to unimaginable heights.

Sometimes, big opportunities might come your way that seem unmissable. You may feel as though you would be crazy to turn them down, however, it is important to first ask yourself a few critical questions:

- What am I hoping to achieve from this?
- Will this decision earn Allāh's pleasure?
- Am I doing it purely for His sake and not to be seen, praised, or recognised by the people?
- Will the worldly or material gain that comes from this potentially harm me spiritually?

If the answers to these questions sit well with you and your conscience feels at peace, then put your trust in Allāh and go ahead. If not, then be brave enough to turn down opportunities that cause your soul to waver and feel content in doing so.

Knowledge is not an inheritance

Within Imam Mālik's family, we observe how, aside from his daughter Fātimah, his other children did not show too much interest in Islamic knowledge or pursuing scholarship. Sometimes there are families of scholars that pass on the baton of learning from one generation to the next. Other times, non-scholarly families produce amazing scholars. Sometimes amazing scholars leave behind children who have no interest in what their parents achieved in life. There are no guarantees in life. Your parent's goodness won't be an automatic pass into a good life for you, neither do their shortcomings have to hold you back.

We are all born into our own unique set of circumstances, and Allāh has given us just the right balance of trials, tragedies, blessings and talents that our soul needs to achieve its mission in life. Understand your true potential and forge your own path. Draw on your 'resource' of the love, support and duʿa of your family to get you there – and if those things are missing in your life, then know that the support of Allāh is never absent.

Imam al-Shāfi'ī

1

Full name: Muḥammad, son of Idrīs, son of al-ʿAbbās, son of ʿUthmān, son of Shāfiʿī, son of al-Ṣā'ib, son of ʿUbayd, son of ʿAbd Yazīd, son of Hāshim, son of al-Muṭṭalib, son of ʿAbd Manāf, al-Ḥijāzī al-Qurashī al-Hāshimī al-Muṭṭalibī

Born in: Gaza, Palestine – 150 AH/767 CE

Died in: Fusṭāṭ, Egypt – 204 AH/820 CE (lived for 54 years)

Best known works: Al-Risālah, Kitāb al-Umm, Musnad al-Shāfiʿī

Difficult beginnings

Tough times had hit Makkah in recent years. The young Idrīs looked to his wife Fātimah and dreamed of providing a more stable life for her and their future family elsewhere. With a heavy heart and uncertain what to expect, Idrīs decided to leave Makkah and head to prosperous Gaza in search of better opportunities. After settling in this region of Sham, to the delight of both parents, they welcomed a beautiful baby boy who they named Muḥammad. Little Muḥammad was less than two years old when tragically, Idrīs passed away leaving behind his wife and son.

Facing the loss of her husband and still unsettled in Gaza, Fātimah needed to make some difficult decisions for her son's future. Should they stay here in Gaza or leave? Where was best to go? Her own family had their roots in Yemen, but she knew it was back home in Makkah that she had more community support and chance of raising her son properly.

With hardly a penny to her name and, still nursing the grief of losing her husband, Fātimah returned to Makkah. Her two-year-old son, Muḥammad, was all she had now. Being left a widow with an orphan child was a huge challenge in Fātimah's society. There was no safety net to help with basic needs and it was not uncommon for this mother and son to live from one meal to the next.

Despite facing extreme poverty, Fātimah had high aspirations for her son. She wanted him to study Islamic knowledge and was willing to do whatever it took to make this easy for him.

Scraping together the very little money she had, Fātimah en-

rolled her son into a small elementary school where he would have the opportunity to learn Qur'an as well as basic reading and writing. The fees for the school used up most of her money, but Fātimah prioritised her son's education over everything else. Living among tent-dwellers in Makkah, Fātimah's son faced such extreme poverty that they could not even afford paper to write on. Young Muḥammad was known to write on stones and bones instead. In their humble home, Fātimah and her son got used to scarce material comforts and barely covering their basic needs, but Fātimah understood why she was making this sacrifice.

After picking her son up from school one day, Muḥammad's teacher gestured for his mum to come and speak with him. *"I'm sorry,"* he began, *"but it is not permissible for me to take any money from you."* [50] Fātimah's heart pounded as she tried to make sense of what he was saying. Her son's teacher continued, explaining that her son was so gifted and was so clearly excelling in school that they were honoured to have a student like him, and did not wish to accept fees for his time in their school.

Fātimah was overcome with relief and also wonder. She always knew her son was special, but to hear the extent of how much he had caught the attention of his teachers was the confirmation her heart needed. She felt reassured that she had made the right decision to place his education as their focus in life.

As an adult, her son would recall: *"When I was in Qur'an school, I would hear the teacher reciting the verses of Qur'an that students needed to memorise, and by the time the teacher had finished reciting the portion, I had already memorised it in its entirety."*

At the tender age of 7, Fātimah's son Muḥammad had completed his memorisation of the Qur'an cover to cover, and his thirst for knowledge grew stronger. Fātimah's lofty ambitions for her son were being realised, as she held fast to her dreams of seeing her son reach his highest potential.

---

[50] Ibn Asākir, *Tārīkh Dimashq*, Dār al-Kutub al-'Ilmīyah, 2012, Vol 51, p 279.

The mothers who raised scholars

Fātimah's commitment to her son was not altogether unique. In our tradition, we have a long line of women who - against all odds - poured everything they had into raising some of the most pioneering scholars of history.

These include:

- Ṣafiyyah bint ʿAbd al-Muṭṭalib single-handedly raised the extraordinary Companion of the Prophet ﷺ, al-Zubayr ibn al-ʿAwwām to become one of the greats of his time.

- Asmā' bint ʿUmays lost her husband in the Battle of Mu'tah but was not deterred in raising her son ʿAbdullāh ibn Jaʿfar to be considered one of the most noble of the youth.

- Hind bint ʿUtbah influenced many of the traits of her prolific son, leader, master strategist and scribe of the Prophet ﷺ Muʿāwiyah ibn Abī Sufyān. So much so, that her son would often introduce himself by proudly declaring, *"I am the son of Hind!". (Ansāb al-Ashrāf)*

- The great leader ʿAbd al-Raḥmān al-Nāṣir marched his army to al-Andalus during a period of great turmoil and chaos. Though his father and uncle were killed when he was a child, his mother never tired from encouraging her son to work harder and go further.

- The mother of the great Sufyān al-Thawrī (known as the 'Leader of the Believers in hadith') made sure to nurture her son's passions and skills at all costs. She frequently reassured him that he always had her support, saying: *"My son, pursue knowledge and I will finance you through my weaving." (Ṣafwat al-Ṣafwah)*

Decisive decades in the desert

Having realised her son's keen interest in Islamic sciences and his promising future, Fātima decided to send her son away to gain the key to unlock it all: the Arabic language. Realising the importance of this step for her son, Fātimah sent her son to travel with the Arab Bedouins so he could master his command of the Arabic language and experience it in its purest, most uncorrupted form.

The young Muḥammad however, didn't just accompany any tribe, he was paired with the esteemed Arab tribe of Hudhayl for this next phase of his journey to knowledge. Hudhayl were known for their talented poets and intellectuals and their reputation for mastery of language had spread far and wide. Muḥammad spent the next 20 years of his life travelling and residing with Hudhayl and during this time, perfected the purest of classical Arabic, memorised vast volumes of poetry and learnt the elaborate ancestries of the tribes of his people. As well as the intellectual strength Muḥammad was gaining while with Hudhayl, he also accessed the subtleties of character and the most valuable qualities of virtue, honour and integrity from their example.

Muḥammad enjoyed many outdoor pursuits too, and during this time with the tribe of Hudhayl, he mastered archery and excelled in horse-riding. His thirst for knowledge and natural curiosity led him to study the field of medicine and learn a great deal about the human body and health.

Those decades immersed in the life and learning of the Bedouins set Muḥammad apart from his peers. Upon his return to Makkah, Muḥammad was not only a master linguist, but had memorised over 10,000 couplets of poetry. He was able to narrate the varied mannerisms of the Arabs, as well as their ancestries and stories. Muḥammad was distinguished in almost every way, however – like Imam Abū Ḥanīfah – a chance encounter and a few words were due to change everything.

A nudge in a new direction

A man from the tribe of ʿUthmān came across Muḥammad one day and swiftly took him aside to give him some sincere advice: "*O Abū ʿAbdullāh* [see: What is a kunyah?], *it really does pain me that this mastery of language that you have, along with your eloquence and intelligence, will pass without mixing it with some fiqh (Islamic law).* *If you were to combine these two, you will* *lead the people of your time."* [51]

Intrigued, Muḥammad asked him, *"Who else is left from the scholars that I should seek knowledge from?"*

The man replied, *"The great man, Mālik ibn Anas, the leader of the Muslims."*

This statement had an immediate and profound effect on Muḥammad. He wasted no time in borrowing a copy of Imam Mālik's book *al-Muwaṭṭa'* and took only nine days to complete memorising it. He wanted to access Imam Mālik, but knew he needed to turn up prepared.

For somebody with the memory of Muḥammad, memorising the *Muwaṭṭa'* was the easy part – now remained the question of how to meet Imam Mālik and learn from him. Imam Mālik was hugely revered, and it would not be as straightforward as simply turning up and asking Imam Mālik to become his teacher.

Approaching the door of Imam Mālik

The reputation of the great Imam Mālik was known to everybody in Makkah and Madinah. Contacting him directly would not be an easy task, but the hunger for knowledge had been kindled within Muḥammad and he was determined.

As the initial step, Muḥammad visited the governor of Makkah to get a written reference that could be passed on to the governor of Madinah. With this reference in hand, Muḥammad travelled to Madinah and met with the governor, asking him to pass on this reference to Imam Mālik – in the hope it would be enough for Imam Mālik to adopt him as a student. After reading the reference, the governor of Madinah sighed and said:

"Young man, by Allāh, walking from the middle of Madinah to the middle of Makkah barefoot is easier for me than approaching the door of Imam Mālik. The only time I have ever felt humiliated is when I stand there."

The status of Imam Mālik was far greater than any of the government officials or even the Caliphs of the time. Unaware of how much awe others had for Imam Mālik, Muḥammad innocently suggested, *"You do not have to go to him, make him come to you."*

Immediately, the governor exclaimed, *"That can never happen! I have no guarantee that even if I, my entourage and you were to ride to his house in a humbled state, that he would even let us in!"*

[51] Abi Abdullah Yaqut ibn Abdullah al-Rumi al-Hamawi, Mu'jam al-Udaba', Dār al-Kutub al-'Ilmīyah, 1991, Vol 6, p 2395.

Undeterred, Muḥammad continued to insist that they at least try, and after much deliberation, the nervous pair found themselves at the door of Imam Mālik's house. They knocked cautiously as Imam Mālik's servant answered.

"Salām and greetings," the governor began, *"I would appreciate it if you could please let Imam Mālik know that the governor of Madinah is at his door and would like to see him."* The servant nodded and went back inside to convey the message. A great deal of time seemed to go by, with the governor and Muḥammad left anxiously wondering what the response would be.

Eventually the servant returned and carefully said, *"He conveys his salām to you and says that if you have a religious question, write it down on a piece of paper and he will answer it. If you want to learn hadith, you should go to his circles of knowledge."*

The governor of Madinah immediately responded, *"Please tell him I have a letter for him from the governor of Makkah, on a very important matter." "Very well,"* the servant replied and went back inside. This time, she returned with a chair. Muḥammad and the governor watched her place it down, unsure what was to happen next.

Suddenly, an imposing tall man with blonde hair, green eyes and fair skin appeared. He looked completely unlike the people of Madinah and without saying a word, sat down on the chair. Feeling unsure, the governor handed him the letter and watched in anticipation as he read it.

Imam Mālik's eyes scanned the letter and then he did something nobody expected, he tossed it aside, saying: *"Subḥān Allāh! Has it come to this? That the knowledge of the Prophet ﷺ now needs connections?"*

The governor found himself lost for words, so Muḥammad jumped in, *"May Allāh bless you, I am a student, from the lineage of the Prophet ﷺ..."* and went on to introduce himself. Imam Mālik listened carefully and when the young man had finished, he asked, *"What is your name?"* Imam al-Shāfiʿī replied, *"Muḥammad."* Imam Mālik then advised him, *"O Muḥammad, be cautious of Allāh and stay away from sins, for you are going to achieve great things. Allāh has placed light in your heart, so do not extinguish it with sins."*

After issuing his advice, Imam Mālik said, *"With pleasure, I will teach you. Come back tomorrow morning, together with someone who can read the Muwaṭṭa' for you."* Muḥammad replied, *"I will read it directly to you."* And this is the very thing he did the following morning.

Bright and early, Muḥammad arrived holding a copy of the *Muwaṭṭa'* in his hand. While his teacher waited for him to open it and begin reading, Muḥammad began reciting the entire book from memory – page by page, chapter by chapter. The great Imam Mālik listened in quiet awe. This young man – with flawless Arabic grammar and eloquent speech – stunned him with his brilliance and Imam Mālik knew he had truly unearthed a gem. When Muḥammad took a pause, Imam Mālik would encourage him to continue, saying *"I ask you, in Allāh's name, keep reading."*

In a number of recitals over a few days, Muḥammad completed his recitation of the Muwaṭṭa' to the very man who wrote it. From that day onwards, Muḥammad remained at the side of Imam Mālik – both in knowledge and service – until his beloved teacher left this world.

Imam al-Shāfi'ī's attitude towards knowledge

Seeking knowledge was a heavy responsibility for the scholars of Islam. Though it certainly was a privilege, it also meant they had to sacrifice their wealth, health, and even lives. Even through this, their love for what they did shone through.

When Imam al-Shāfiʿī was once asked, *"Describe to us your craving for knowledge,"* he replied: *"At times I hear a piece of knowledge that I had not heard of before, and so I wish that the rest of my limbs (arms and legs) had ears so that they could experience the pleasure that my ears had just experienced."*

Tawāliʿ al-Ta'sīs

Standing firm against scheming in Yemen

After the devastating death of his beloved teacher, Muḥammad had grown in knowledge and recognition, and was now referred to as Imam al-Shāfiʿī. He made his way back from Madinah to Makkah. Here, he wed his wife Ḥamīdah bint Nāfiʿ, the granddaughter of the third Caliph ʿUthmān ibn ʿAffān. The couple shared two sons and a daughter: Abū ʿUthmān, Abū'l-Ḥasan and Fātimah (named after his beloved mother).

As he settled back into life in Makkah with his family, Imam al-Shāfiʿī was approached by the governor of Yemen who requested his service in Yemen. Al-Shāfiʿī agreed to this and became governor of Najran, issuing rulings with justice and ethics. For those who wanted to evade the law and continue in their corrupt ways, the presence of Imam al-Shāfiʿī amongst them was becoming quite a nuisance. A group of nine men came together and, in the darkness of the night, hatched a plot to incriminate al-Shāfiʿī and destroy his reputation. They all created a long list of false accusations and made sure their stories matched up.

Feeling confident that there were enough of them to convince the Caliph of Baghdad that their newly appointed governor of Najran was dangerous and should be immediately removed from his position, the men entered the court of Hārūn al-Rashīd.

One by one, they began their list of elaborate and damning lies against Imam al-Shāfiʿī – each one growing more and more destructive. They encouraged one another to fiercely tear apart the reputation of Imam al-Shāfiʿī and felt certain their character assassination would convince their audience.

Imam al-Shāfiʿī was also present in the court. He sat alone and listened calmly as he witnessed the men invent dark and wicked allegations against him, yet did not speak until he was invited to. When given his turn, Imam al-Shāfiʿī argued his defence with eloquence, honesty and integrity. The power of his arguments spoke for themselves, his powerful delivery of them was merely the cherry on top.

After listening intently to both sides of the court, the Caliph Hārūn al-Rashīd was hugely moved and notably impressed by al-Shāfiʿī. It took no time for his innocence to be declared and for the nine men who schemed and plotted to face punishment for the lies they peddled so enthusiastically.

The travels of Imam al-Shāfiʿī

True to his priorities, while in Yemen Imam al-Shāfiʿī immersed himself in the scholarly circles at every opportunity. He sat with, discussed, and learnt from many teachers in Yemen before making his way to Baghdad in Iraq. In Iraq, Imam al-Shāfiʿī would encounter somebody who would bring untold benefit on his path to learning, Muḥammad ibn al-Ḥasan al-Shaybānī, one of the chief students of Imam Abū Ḥanīfah in Baghdad.

The meeting of these two men, mountains in their own right, helped to add another generous layer of understanding to Imam al-Shāfiʿī's vast field of knowledge and continued to expand his horizons. Imam al-Shāfiʿī always welcomed the opportunity to expose himself to new teachers and ways of understanding and this meeting with Muḥammad ibn al-Ḥasan was no exception to that.

He said himself: *"I have amassed a camel's load of knowledge from Muḥammad ibn al-Ḥasan, which I heard directly from him."* [52]

[52] Al-Dhahabī, *Siyar Aʿlām al-Nubalā',* Dār al-Kutub al-'Ilmīyah, Vol 8, p 240.

What the scholars said about al-Shāfiʿī

Abū Thawr said: "I have never seen a person like al-Shāfiʿī, nor has he ever seen a person like himself." (Shadharat al-Dhahab)

Muḥammad ibn ʿAbd al-Ḥakam said: *"The students of hadith would come to al-Shāfiʿī and ask him about the most intricate matters. He would guide them to secrets of knowledge that they had not heard before, and they would leave amazed. Similarly, the students of fiqh – both those who agreed and disagreed with him – would leave his gatherings in a state of humility. In the same vein, the students of language would present him with poetry, which he would decode for them." (Mir'āt al-Jinān)*

Yūnus ibn ʿAbd al-Aʿlā said of his productivity: *"Al-Shāfiʿī would complete the authoring of a book between the early morning hours and noon." (Ṭawāliʿ al-Ta'sīs)*

We often hear about the benefits of travel and how it helps to broaden a person's mind. This was never truer than for Imam al-Shāfiʿī who would be regarded as well travelled, even by modern standards. Following his stay in Iraq, Imam al-Shāfiʿī journeyed to Egypt.

Honouring different opinions

Imam al-Shāfiʿī was born in the same year that Imam Abu Hanifa died, so he never got to meet this great scholar. Imam al-Shāfiʿī had studied the works and opinions of Imam Abū Ḥanīfah and knew them well. One day, he was praying at a mosque very close to the grave of Imam Abū Ḥanīfah. Imam al-Shāfiʿī believed that during prayer, one should raise their hands every time they say the takbīr ('Allāhu akbar'), but this was not the view of Imam Abū Ḥanīfah. When Imam al-Shāfiʿī prayed at this mosque, the people around him noticed that he did not raise his hands during prayer as he normally did. When people asked him after his prayer why he chose to pray that way, he gestured towards where Imam Abū Ḥanīfah was buried, and said, *"I did that out of respect to the owner of the grave."*

This showed how much respect Imam al-Shāfi'ī had for Imam Abū Ḥanīfah and that their different opinions were not seen as a problem. He had the humility to adjust his prayer actions to something he wouldn't normally do, because he wanted to honour the opinion of Imam Abū Ḥanīfah, who he held in the highest regard.

How Imam al-Shāfi'ī worshipped

For a man so regarded for his keen intelligence and incredible wisdom, Imam al-Shāfi'ī understood the needs of his soul more than anyone. This was reflected in the devotion he had to worship, something that only increased with his knowledge.

One of the most well-known students of Imam al-Shāfi'ī observed him complete the recitation of the Qur'an a staggering sixty times in the month of Ramadan. Outside of Ramadan, the majority of al-Shāfi'ī's Qur'an recitation would be during his long night prayers before dawn. The same student, al-Rabī' said, *"Al-Shāfi'ī divided his night into three parts: the first third for writing, the second third for prayer and the final third for sleep."*

When it came to enjoying the finest food available to him, al-Shāfi'ī said of himself: *"I have not eaten to my full for the last 16 years.... This is because being full causes laziness, hardens the heart, limits sharpness, brings sleepiness and weakens worship."* [53]

Though not frail or elderly, Imam al-Shāfi'ī bewildered others by his habit of walking with a walking stick. Asked to explain, he said it was, *"so that I always remember that I am a traveller,"* [54] because a staff is often used by people trekking long distances.

The reputation of al-Shāfi'ī had spread far and wide, not least to the numerous places he had visited. Though as his fame and prestige grew, al-Shāfi'ī made sure to exercise humility at all costs, saying: *"The highest person in status is the one who believes he has none, and the most virtuous of all people is the one who believes he has none."* [55]

---

[53] Al-Dhahabī, *Siyar A'lām al-Nubalā',* Dār al-Kutub al-'Ilmīyah, Vol 8, p 248.
[54] Al-Dhahabī, *Siyar A'lām al-Nubalā',* Dār al-Kutub al-'Ilmīyah, Vol 8, p 279.
[55] Al-Dhahabī, Siyar *A'lām al-Nubalā',* Dār al-Kutub al-'Ilmīyah, Vol 8, p 280.

Signs we need to work on our humility

Though Imam al-Shāfiʿī benefitted his society, and all of the Muslim Ummah since, with an unrivalled contribution to Islamic learning, he knew that pride and self-admiration would destroy it all. He was extra vigilant to watch out for signs that his ego and pride were getting the better of him.

Some of the signs of ego we should look out for within ourselves are:

- Struggling to accept advice.
- Refusing to offer an apology.
- Refusing to accept an apology.
- Insisting on revenge.
- Refusing to walk away from a heated debate that is not going anywhere.

During his numerous debates, al-Shāfiʿī was never once heard raising his voice and he never once desired to humiliate or 'crush' his opponent. His sincere and compassionate approach to discussion is one that would hardly be recognisable to most people today:

"In every debate of mine, my wish was that Allāh helps and guides my opponent, and I hoped that Allāh would preserve and guard him. In all my debates, I have never cared about whether the truth becomes apparent through me or him, and in all my debates, I have never wanted my opponent to make a mistake, nor did I ever debate anyone for the purpose of overcoming him. The only intention was advice."

Conscious of how easy it is for pride and vanity to slip in and muddy our intentions, Imam al-Shāfiʿī actually wished to avoid his name being mentioned at all: *"I wish that people could have learnt this knowledge without any of it being attributed to me, hence Allāh would reward me without the need for people's praise."*[56]

Knowledge from many fields

Imam al-Shāfiʿī understood the benefit of learning from as wide a variety of fields as possible, for a broad and balanced view of the world.

He would say:

"Whoever learns the Qur'an, his worth increases,

Whoever studies fiqh, his status increases,

Whoever studies the Arabic language, his demeanour softens,

Whoever studies mathematics, his opinions become precise,

Whoever writes hadith, his arguments become strong,

Whoever does not guard himself from sins, his knowledge will be of no use to him."

Tārīkh Baghdād

[56] Al-Dhahabī, Siyar Aʿlām al-Nubalā', Dār al-Kutub al-'Ilmīyah, Vol 8, p 245.

Leaving this world as a throne of gold awaits...

The Steps to Knowledge

Before setting out on the path to knowledge, Imam al-Shāfiʿī believed a person should prepare their heart and character first.

He would advise others: "My student, you will never gain knowledge in the absence of six." These are:

- Sharpness
- Eagerness
- Sacrifice
- Means (resources and money)
- The company of a scholar

After Imam al-Shāfiʿī's second visit to Iraq, he decided to travel to Egypt in the year 199 AH. The people of Baghdad were sad to see him go and asked why he had to leave them. Imam al-Shāfiʿī simply replied, *"There (Egypt) will be the place of my dying."*

As soon as Imam al-Shāfiʿī arrived in Egypt, he began to feel unwell, and his health began to decline. More than most people, Imam al-Shāfiʿī knew that time on this earth was limited, precious and slipping away from him. Despite his sickness getting worse, Imam al-Shāfiʿī didn't slow down his teaching or learning. For days and weeks, he continued serving the people as a scholar and persevered in gaining knowledge and committing himself to worship. Eventually, Imam al-Shāfiʿī became weakened to the point where he felt the end of his life was very close.

As he was experiencing the throes of death, one of his students, al-Muzanī, entered and asked, *"How are you, O Imam?"* to which he responded: *"It looks like I will be departing from this world today, leaving my friends and meeting my Lord. I do not know whether my soul will be taken to Paradise so that I should rejoice or driven to Hell so that I should mourn."*

As he was considering what was coming up for him in his journey into the Hereafter, Imam al-Shāfiʿī cried intensely and recited the following couplets of poetry:

"When my heart became hardened and my paths became narrow,
I took my hope in Your pardon as my opening and escape
My sins seemed so great, but when I compared them to your forgiveness,
I found Your forgiveness to be far greater." [57]

Imam al-Shāfiʿī knew that the very end of his life would be the most testing time for him – because how you perfect an action is known at the finish. On the last night of the month of Rajab in the year 820 CE/204 AH in Egypt, the soul of this great man left his body; Imam al-Shāfiʿī returned to his Creator at the age of 54. The governor of Egypt led his funeral prayers, with his sons ʿAbū'l-Hasan and ʿUthmān present. He was buried at the foot of the Muqattam Hills in Cairo, Egypt.

Shortly afterwards, al-Rabīʿ, Imam al-Shāfiʿī's close student said: *"I saw al-Shāfiʿī in a dream after his demise. I said to him, 'O Father of ʿAbdullāh, how did Allāh receive you?' He replied, 'He sat me on a throne of gold and poured over me the purest of pearls.'"* [58]

[57] 57. Al-Dhahabı, *Siyar A'lām al-Nubalā'*, Dār al-Kutub al-'Ilmīyah, Vol 8, p 269.
[58] Abu Bakr Ahmad bin Ali al-Khatīb al-Baghdādi
Tahqiq, Tārīkh Baghdād, Dār al-Kutub al-'Ilmīyah, Vol 2, p 404.

Lessons we can learn

Greatness can often be traced back to the efforts of mothers

Against all odds, Imam al-Shāfiʿī's mother dedicated her energy towards making sure that her son was able to reach his fullest potential. She had to overcome one obstacle after another but did not let this stop her dream for her son. She was a young widow who unexpectedly had to face life as a single mother: a turn of events that she had never prepared for. She was also struggling with money and lived in poverty with a young son to raise. When she was in Gaza, she had no family, friends or connections to support her through her difficulties. Instead, she had a goal, and took practical steps to help achieve it.

When you have a strong intention towards an action pleasing to Allāh, you only have to put your effort in and Allāh will open up a path for you. Sometimes you may feel like you have too many hurdles to overcome, and you can't see how your goal is possible, but it is Allāh who will bring the right people, places and circumstances to you and cause events to unfold in a way you never imagined. The 'life chances' of a young orphan boy in poverty probably did not look too hopeful for Imam al-Shāfiʿī at the time, however, we now know him as one the greatest minds that ever lived. His legacy was made possible through the dedication of his mother. Nobody on earth will care for you and your wellbeing as much as your mother so, even if you struggle to see it sometimes, remember the blessing of a parent who wants you to be the very best you can be.

Seek out and be part of the best company

With no father or extended family around him, it would have been easy for the young Muḥammad to spend time hanging around with people who were not motivated to achieve anything in life. His mother understood that one of the best things she could do for him is to surround him with the best company. She wanted him to learn Islamic knowledge, manners and have an ambition for his life, so she took him to a school, and then to scholars, where he could access this.

Growing up, the company you keep and the friends you have, make up who you are likely to become. You begin to share similar ideas, boundaries and attitudes as the people you spend the most time with, so take a step back and look at your closest companions. Think carefully about the people, places and activities you expose yourself to and whether you feel these things are benefitting you as a person. What we surround ourselves with sets us on a particular course in life, so be sure to have goals and pick your friends wisely to help you achieve them.

Important things deserve preparation

When Imam al-Shāfiʿī decided he wanted to meet Imam Mālik and learn from him, he wasted no time in preparing himself. Without being nudged, he got himself a copy of Imam Mālik's main book al-Muwaṭṭa' and began reading, learning and memorising it. He committed it to memory entirely in nine days. This meant that when he finally came face-to-face with the great (and quite intimidating!) Imam Mālik, he had already done his research and was better prepared to answer his questions and show why he was worthy to become his student.

You do not have to memorise whole books, however, taking proactive steps to prepare yourself for important events shows that you care about your goal and are willing to work hard for it.

If you are meeting a relative or guest for the first time, maybe spare some time with your family to ask about them, their background and their interests beforehand. This will mean you have more to talk about when you see them, and they'll be touched by the effort you made.

The biggest event we can prepare for is our life now and the one to come.

Preparation for this involves learning about the purpose of why we are alive, actions that lead to a better life and about people (like these Four Imams!) who can act as role models to learn from.

Facing betrayal can teach you painful, but necessary lessons

After accepting a role in Yemen, Imam al-Shāfiʿī found himself unpopular with people who didn't want to have their behaviour kept in check by him. They plotted, planned and schemed to put an end to his role and to his freedom too. Through clearly conveying the truth of the situation, Imam al-Shāfiʿī convinced the Caliph he was innocent of the things they accused him of, and he was set free.

Like Imam al-Shāfiʿī, you may also find yourself in a situation where people have wronged you. Through jealousy, hostility or their own deep-seated issues, people in life may not want you to succeed and might even try to work against you. Remain truthful, patient and understand this is a test that is sent to you. Difficult times can bring the heat necessary to mould, strengthen and reshape your character into a much better version of your previous self. Stand up for the truth and justice and understand that all experiences – even the painful and bitter ones – are sent as an opportunity for you to grow and become stronger.

Different perspectives can all be equally valid

One of the unique aspects of Imam al-Shāfiʿī's life was not only how extensively he travelled, but how much he was exposed to the learning and teaching of many different communities and regions. This broad understanding of different perspectives opens up your ability to engage and understand different people's point of view. For Imam al-Shāfiʿī, it allowed him to act as a bridge between two dominant schools of thought (the teachings of Imam Abū Ḥanīfah and Imam Mālik) and reconcile them. Because Imam al-Shāfiʿī studied under Imam Abū Ḥanīfah's most distinguished student (from whom he amassed "a camel's load of knowledge") and also from Imam Mālik directly, he got very familiar with the perspectives of the scholars of both Iraq and Madinah.

This shows us that different perspectives in learning can all be equally valid and important, there need not be an 'either/or' attitude to knowledge. Learning different approaches to knowledge helps you understand your topic deeper and look at the same thing from many different angles. Don't be afraid to explore different ways of learning a topic you might feel you know a lot about already – there is always the chance to broaden your horizons further.

Treat fame, admiration and public adoration with great caution

Imam al-Shāfiʿī was extremely wary of falling into self-admiration as he was worried this would contaminate the purity of his deeds. We know that all our acts of worship should be done only for the pleasure of Allāh, but when you have a lot of people admiring and complimenting you, it is easy to start doing things to be praised by others. Imam al-Shāfiʿī knew he was at risk of this because his reputation had spread so far and wide that most people insisted on treating him like royalty. This made him deeply uncomfortable, and he longed to just be able to teach without having his name identified or spoken of.

It is always important for us to regularly check in on our intentions and make sure that we preserve our acts of worship only for Allāh. This is not always easy because sometimes we might feel some self-pride and admiration creep into our hearts. Always check in on yourself at the beginning, middle and end of actions to ask yourself: "Who am I doing this for? Am I trying to look good in the eyes of other people? Is their praise of me encouraging me to do more?" It is always important to question your inner state and remind yourself that you are doing your actions purely for Allāh and not anyone or anything else.

Never allow yourself to get too confident and complacent about your deeds

There are very few of us that can hope to achieve even a fraction of what Imam al-Shāfiʿī did in his short lifetime. But even though he was one of the best minds to have ever lived, Imam al-Shāfiʿī didn't feel safe and smug while he was on his deathbed. He spoke openly about being unsure how his soul was going to be received by Allāh, and how he hoped he had earned the pleasure of Allāh before he died.

Imam al-Shāfiʿī had this perspective because as he increased in knowledge, he also increased in humility, good character and worship. His learning was constantly affecting his heart and actions, and making him more humble and sincere.

After we do a good deed like give charity or fast, it is easy to feel like we should congratulate ourselves and be proud of our achievements. However, we should try to remember that we were only inspired to do those deeds through Allāh in the first place, so it is a blessing from Him when He gives us the opportunity to do good actions.

Imam Aḥmad

Full name: Aḥmad, son of Muḥammad, son of Ḥanbal, son of Hilāl, son of Asad, son of Idrīs, son of ʿAbdullāh, son of Ḥayyān al-Shaybānī

Born in: Baghdad, Iraq – 164 AH/780 CE

Died in: Baghdad, Iraq – 241 AH/855 CE (lived for 74 years)

Best known works: Musnad Aḥmad ibn Ḥanbal, Al-Radd ʿalā al-Jamiyyah wa'l-Zanādiqah, Kitāb al-Sunnah

Starting out life as an orphan

The early years of young Aḥmad's life had already seen more upheaval than most people he knew. The son of a soldier, Aḥmad's father was killed on the battlefield while still in his thirties, and this left Aḥmad alone in the care of his mother. Ṣafiyyah bint Maymūnah was no ordinary woman however, she understood that setbacks in life only meant striving harder and rising stronger. Despite being a young widow, Ṣafiyyah refused to succumb to a fate of low aspirations and simply trying to get by. She had a vision for her son, and it was greater than their circumstances at the time.

Like the widowed mother of orphaned Imam al-Shāfiʿī, Ṣafiyyah decided she was going to dedicate her life to raising her son well and poured all her energy into this singular aim. As his first teacher, Aḥmad's mother nurtured his love for Allāh and tenderly encouraged the regular discipline of prayer and Qur'an recitation. It is difficult to imagine young people today being immersed in long acts of worship however those close to young Aḥmad, like Ibrāhīm ibn Shammās, would report:

"I knew Aḥmad ibn Ḥanbal when he was a boy, and he would spend the night in prayer." [59]

---

[59] Ibn al-Jawzī, *Ṣifat al-Ṣafwa*, Dar al-Ghad al-Jadeed, Vol 1, p 483.

By the time he reached his teenage years, Aḥmad had already memorised the entire Qur'an and made the conscious decision that he would dedicate the rest of his life to seeking beneficial knowledge. As the last of the Four Imams, Aḥmad had the advantage of their examples and legacy to draw upon in his own life as well as their students. As it was, Imam Abū Yūsuf (who was one of the main students of Imam Abū Ḥanīfah) became one of Aḥmad's first teachers.

As Aḥmad grew, he attended the study circles of many teachers, however one thing that remained consistent through the years would be how the young man prepared for his lessons. When classes were held directly after *Fajr* prayer, he would wake up hours before dawn and leave during the hours of darkness. Concerned for her son, Aḥmad's mother would often plead with him to at least wait for the call to prayer to begin before leaving home.

During a time where Aḥmad was eagerly absorbing all the knowledge his teachers had, he found one of the great hadith teachers, Hushaym ibn Bashīr, and became his most loyal student. For four years, Aḥmad stuck to Hushaym's side and eagerly memorised everything his teacher instructed him to. [60] When Hushaym sadly passed away, Aḥmad found himself at a crossroads in his life. He had sat in most of the study circles of Baghdad, yet his appetite to know more was only growing. A new chapter began in young Aḥmad's life, one marked with eager travel in the pursuit of knowledge.

Onto journeys far from home with Yahyā

Within a few days of Hushaym's death, Aḥmad packed his bags and set off on a quest into the unknown. However, he took more than just his belongings with him, joining him was his lifelong friend and study-mate Yaḥyā ibn Maʿīn. Together, Aḥmad and Yaḥyā travelled to Kufa with the understanding that the journey they were on would come with many sacrifices and tests of sincerity. The financial strain upon these two young men was so great that they would use a piece of masonry as a pillow to rest on at night. Following on from Kufa, the pair travelled within Iraq to Basra and then Wasit.

Exhausting the study circles of the cities, they then went further afield, travelling to Makkah, Madinah, Yemen and Persia. In Makkah, Ahmad got the opportunity to meet with fellow heavyweight Imam al-Shāfiʿī and took great delight in this honour. Aḥmad longed for the opportunity to meet Imam Mālik, but despite

[60] Ibn al-Jawzī, Ṣifat al-Ṣafwa, Dar al-Ghad al-Jadeed, Vol 2, p 9.

his best efforts, this was not decreed for him.

In the year 198 AH, Aḥmad and Yaḥyā planned for the next phase of their journey together. They were going to head out towards Makkah and perform hajj. From hajj, they planned to set off for Yemen to meet and study under the great scholar ʿAbd al-Razzāq. While in the throngs of the crowd during *ṭawāf,* the two men were shocked to come face to face with ʿAbd al-Razzāq himself. After greeting one another, ʿAbd al-Razzāq began: *"I have heard such great things about you Aḥmad, what an honour this is!"*

Yaḥyā saw a great opportunity ahead and said, *"Why don't we study from ʿAbd al-Razzāq right here in Makkah since we are all here, we can avoid the long and tiring journey to Yemen!"* Aḥmad was not on board however, *"No, Yaḥyā, I have made an intention to travel to Yemen to seek knowledge and I won't alter it now. Whatever we must learn from ʿAbd al-Razzāq and others, we will take from their knowledge there."*

With that, they concluded hajj and set off for Yemen. During the exhausting journey - as often happened - their finances ran dry. Despite being considered a scholar with a growing reputation, Aḥmad had no hesitation in earning money through halal means and found work carrying other people's luggage. Aḥmad refused to take money off anybody else and made sure he was self-sufficient with his earnings, despite the difficult position it put him in. His poverty reached such an extreme that at one point, he was forced to pawn his own shoes to a baker in return for some bread.

These exertions were not for nothing however, as Aḥmad had a clear goal in mind. Travelling over dozens of countries led to the compilation of his most famous work: the *Musnad*. Aḥmad had originally collected a total of over 750,000 hadith, which he then whittled down. The *Musnad* became a shortened compilation of 40,000 narrations from the Prophet ﷺ that he learned personally from his teachers around the globe. Now known as Imam Aḥmad, his travels were so prolific that later, even great scholars like Ibn Jawzī acknowledged,

"He (Aḥmad) travelled the world twice until he compiled his Musnad." [61]

[61] Ibn al-Jawzī, Sayd al-Khāir, Dar Us-Sunnah Classic Collection, Vol 1, p 259.

The character of Imam Aḥmad

His refusal to accept favours

Imam Aḥmad had very strong principles and one thing which was particularly important to him was to always be self-sufficient, and never receive favours from others. This often pushed him to the depth of poverty, yet he didn't relent. He refused to accept the many loans or gifts that others were eager to give him, including from family, friends, teachers, students or even wealthy Muslim leaders!

One of his teachers, Yazīd ibn Hārūn, would regularly support his students financially and most of them gratefully accepted this support, including Aḥmad's close friend Yaḥyā. Aḥmad on the other hand, was the only student who refused to accept even a dirham from Yazīd.

Aḥmad's entire income came from renting out a property he had inherited from his father. This wasn't a reliable income stream and left Aḥmad in regular financial hardship. Aḥmad didn't allow this to slow down his ambitions and he pushed through his circumstances to achieve his aims. He performed hajj five times, three of these journeys were done on foot due to his poverty. According to his own account, he spent only thirty dirhams (one dirham would typically buy you a chicken and is equivalent to 2.975 grams of silver) during one of these trips.

The writing on the wall

ʿAlī ibn al-Jahm tells us a story which summarises Imam Aḥmad's dedication to self-sufficiency: *"I had a neighbour who pulled out a manuscript and said: 'Do you know whose handwriting this is?' We said: 'Yes, it is that of Aḥmad ibn Ḥanbal, how did you get it?'*

He told us: 'We were in Makkah studying when Aḥmad ibn Ḥanbal joined us for a while then suddenly disappeared. Concerned, we made our way to his house to check everything was okay with him. When we got there and entered his home, we saw he was wearing just two pieces of clothing, far less than normal. We asked him what happened, and he told us his clothes had been stolen.

'I then insisted he take some money from me as a loan or a gift, just to replace his clothes. Aḥmad strongly refused this offer. So, then I had to think hard and finally said: "Write some knowledge for me and I will pay you." This Aḥmad accepted. When I took out a dinar of gold, Aḥmad once again refused to take so much. He told me to go and buy a pen and paper and bring back the change as his payment, which is what I did. This is why I have a manuscript here in my home written in his noble handwriting.'" [62]

His interactions with the people

Each of the Four Imams were individuals, with unique personality traits that defined them. One of the strongest features of Imam Aḥmad's character was his immense compassion for the poor. Despite struggling financially himself, he was always incredibly generous with the little that he possessed. He would make people feel special and lift the spirits of the downtrodden in society by remembering and addressing them by their favourite nicknames. When people met him, he would greet them with delight and attention. In the presence of teachers, he instantly humbled himself, though ironically, it was often the scholars themselves who revered him.

[62] Imam Abu Nu'aym al-Asbahani, *Ḥilyat al- Awliyā',* *Dār al-Kutub al-'Ilmīyah*, Vol 9, p 177.

Why was Imam Aḥmad so strongly committed to being self-sufficient?

When you read about the poverty that Imam Aḥmad struggled through, it may appear extreme or rigid to be so averse to accepting help. Where did this motivation come from? Imam Aḥmad's choice was inspired by narrations like that of ʿAwf ibn Mālik, a Companion of the Prophet ﷺ who, together with nine others, pledged allegiance to the Prophet ﷺ.

When the Companions asked the Prophet ﷺ what the conditions of this pledge were, the Messenger of Allāh ﷺ replied:
"That you worship Allāh without associating partners with Him, pray five times and obey Allāh."

The Prophet ﷺ then lowered his voice and mentioned another clause discreetly, saying: *"And that you do not ask people for anything."*

ʿAwf said: *"After this, I saw some of the Companions not asking anyone for help even to pick up their whip if it had fallen from their hands."*

(Muslim)

His humility

As has been a strong running theme with all the Imams we have covered, Imam Aḥmad was known for his impeccable manners, to the extent that his students were fixated on them. It was said by Ismāʿīl ibn ʿUlayyah:

"There were around 5000 students or more in Aḥmad's classes, 500 of whom were writing, whilst the remainder were learning from his manners." [63]

Part of Aḥmad's manners was his utmost humility, never considering himself superior to anyone else, even his students. He was known to frequently look

[63] Al-Dhahabī, Siyar Aʿlām al-Nubalāʾ
Dār al-Kutub al-ʿIlmīyah, Vol 11, p 316.

down at the ground and when he was around non-Arabs, he felt no superiority over them.

His friend Yaḥyā recalled: *"I have never seen anyone greater than Aḥmad. Never did he see himself as being above us because he was an Arab, and he never once brought it up."*

In fact, when Aḥmad himself was asked whether or not he was an Arab at all, he responded: *"We are a people to be pitied."*

Aḥmad's humility reached so far that he was puzzled when people would ask him to make du'a for them. A neighbour of Aḥmad's, 'Alī ibn Abī Fazārah, tells us about an incident where he sought Imam Aḥmad's help for his mother:

"My mother suffered from paralysis for around 20 years. She once said to me: *'Go to Aḥmad ibn Ḥanbal and ask him to make du'a for me.'* So, I made my way to his house and knocked on his door. He said: *'Who is it?'* I replied, *'Your neighbour. My mother is an old and disabled woman. She has asked me to request your du'a for her.'* I heard him mumble words of confusion, saying: *'I am in more need for her du'a than she is of mine!'*

I was about to make my way back home when Imam Aḥmad's door suddenly opened. It was an old woman asking me if I was the one who was just speaking to Imam Aḥmad. I confirmed I was, and she told me *'I just left him as he was making du'a for your mother.'* Rushing home with this news, I knocked on my mother's front door. The door opened and my mother was standing there on her own two feet.

She beamed as she said: *'Allāh has gifted me with wellbeing!'"*[64]

Part of Imam Aḥmad's manners would be to respect the time and efforts of anybody who visited his home. He would take note of the names of each visitor and make a point to return the visit.

One time, when an excited visitor said to him, *"May Allāh reward you for everything that you have done for Islam"*, Imam Aḥmad immediately became agitated and responded: *"Rather, may Allāh reward Islam for what it has done for me! Who am I? Who am I?"*

---

[64] Ibn al-Jawzī, Ṣifat al-Ṣafwa, Dar al-Ghad al-Jadeed, Vol 1, p 485.

His dedication to worship

Though lenient and light-hearted with the people, Imam Aḥmad was extremely disciplined and serious about his personal worship. From the very earliest age, Aḥmad's commitment to worship was recognised amongst the people and as his scholarly credentials grew, his personal worship only continued to increase alongside it.

With a reputation that began in his adolescent years, Imam Aḥmad grew to become one of the greatest worshippers of his era. He went from a peak of praying over 300 *rakʿah* of prayer a day to the most testing time in his life when – during his 70s – he was only able to pray 150 *rakʿahs*. He would complete the recitation of the Qur'an once a week and would routinely forego a full night's sleep so he could remain awake for prayer. His regular habit would be to take a short nap after *ʿIshā'* prayer and remain awake in prayer until *Fajr* time.

Putting his knowledge into practice

One defining feature of Imam Aḥmad was his enthusiasm to practically apply every bit of knowledge he had acquired. He said himself: *"There is not a hadith that I have written down except that I first applied its teaching."*

Out of respect for the Sunnah of the Prophet ﷺ, Imam Aḥmad only began teaching at the age of 40, arguing that this was the age that the Prophet ﷺ received prophethood.

Imam Aḥmad knew the life he was pursuing was not average. For him to be successful in spreading sacred knowledge, he would have to raise his own standards of conduct, worship and outlook accordingly. Making sure he applied what he learnt had a transformative effect on Imam Aḥmad, as he would never teach something without making sure he had fully implemented it into his own life. To this end, the great Ḥasan al-Baṣrī described the impact that learning would have on a person:

"In the past, when a person would start their journey to knowledge, the effects of his learning would begin appearing in his glances, words, hands, prayer, humility and minimalism." [65]

In today's terms, Imam Aḥmad didn't just talk the talk, but very much walked the walk too. Learning abstract knowledge is easy and without practical action, it can become a career or pastime that one dips in and out of. Imam Aḥmad

---

[65] Imam Abdullah Ibn al-Mubārak, *Kitab al-Zuhd & Kitab Ar-Raqa'iq*, Dār al-Kutub al-'Ilmīyah, Vol 1, p 26.

however, understood that the knowledge he was acquiring had a right upon him, and that it was to be implemented and applied practically. This is easier said than done and often leads to a person learning at a much slower pace. However, to go slowly and sincerely is much better than to speed through knowledge and remain unchanged in your character.

His willingness to say "I don't know"

Like all the great scholars, most notably his contemporary Imam Mālik, Imam Aḥmad had deep reservations about answering questions on any matters that he wasn't completely sure about. Though he had acquired more knowledge than most people alive at his time, this did not give him boldness and enthusiasm to share his opinions. Rather, it instilled caution and humility in his speech.

People would travel from far and wide to pose their questions to Imam Aḥmad. To be able to get in front of the Imam with a question was considered a privilege in and of itself. Imagine then, the surprise of many questioners when the Imam simply declared "I don't know" as a response.

The bar for certainty was so high for Imam Aḥmad that he would never feel tempted to guess an answer or give his closest opinion on a topic without absolute certainty. Imam Aḥmad was never willing to speak without knowledge on religious affairs, and soon became increasingly creative in rebuffing questions he did not feel comfortable answering. This is not to say that Imam Aḥmad turned people away in confusion and doubt about what to do, they would have their own local teachers to consult for advice. Imam Aḥmad merely turned them away from getting a confident answer from him if he wasn't absolutely sure of what he was saying.

Alternative ways of saying "I don't know" used by Imam Aḥmad

When unsure of a question, Imam Aḥmad was known to use a variety of statements in response:

- "I have not heard anything in this regard."
- "I do not issue rulings on this."
- "I do not have the courage to speak of it."
- "I do not have an answer."
- "I fear answering this question."
- "It is an unclear matter."
- "The scholars have differed."
- "Ask the scholars."
- "It terrifies me."
- "It is an intricate topic."

Being troubled by fame

Imam Aḥmad was extremely troubled by the heights of fame he had reached. His reputation was rapidly growing and with it, so was his dread. He viewed fame with a great deal of caution and understood the danger it can pose to a person's sincerity. The risk of being so well known is that you could begin to have pride, arrogance or ego enter your heart, even if it begins as the smallest seed. Desiring fame and to be admired by the people were always seen as *diseases of the heart*, and something that can destroy your intention to do good for Allāh's sake alone.

Imam Aḥmad's unease with fame was so great that he said: *"I want to live in a remote valley in Makkah where no one will recognise me. I have been afflicted with fame. I desire death every morning and evening."* [66]

[66] Al-Dhahabi, Siyar Aʿlām al-Nubalāʾ, Dār al-Kutub al-ʿIlmīyah, Vol 11, p 216.

When someone once said to him, *"There are so many people making du'a for you!",* rather than feeling comforted, his eyes flooded with tears as he said, *"I am afraid that this is a sign of me being baited into destruction."*

What he meant by this was that by being told that *'so many'* people were making *du'a* for him, it might lead him to start believing he was that important, famous and worthy of admiration – and those qualities would destroy his character and deeds.

All the scholars of our tradition were extremely wary of the consequence of fame and becoming popular. They would want to guard their sincerity so strongly that they preferred acts of worship done privately, with only Allāh's knowledge of it. Our deeds are only as good as the intention they began with, so if a person corrupts their intention from the beginning (by doing an action just to look good in front of others), it has made all their subsequent actions null and void in the sight of Allāh. The scholars would avoid fame to preserve and have their life's work accepted by Allāh as worthy of reward.

Where is Ibrāhīm ibn Adham?

The great Imam Ibrāhīm ibn Adham once left his hometown and travelled to another city, entering one of its gardens. News quickly spread that the Imam – known for his piety and religiosity – was in town and had just entered the garden.

Immediately a huge throng of people from the city gathered and rushed into the garden to catch sight of Imam Ibrāhīm, someone who they had never seen before, but had heard amazing things about.

The people jostled around the garden and frantically began to question one another: *"Where is Ibrāhīm ibn Adham? Where is Ibrāhīm ibn Adham?"*

Ibrāhīm ibn Adham, witnessing this spectacle, made the decision to walk around with them saying, *"Where is Ibrāhīm ibn Adham?"*

Imam Ibrāhīm joined a long line of scholars who believed that seeking and desiring fame was something to always remain on guard against.

The greatest trial of Imam Ahmad's life

Though Imam Aḥmad had lived a full, rich and deep life, nothing he experienced would prepare him for the most challenging trial of his life. This would be a matter that would test every ounce of resolve and courage Imam Aḥmad had and test the strength of his character in a way nothing else had. It would also cost him 17 years of his life and put him through a level of physical, mental and emotional torture that he could never had imagined. In many ways, everything that Imam Aḥmad experienced in his life was a preparation for this chapter in his life, and he would have to draw upon his knowledge, sincerity and bravery to see it through.

What was the 'trial'?

As it was the very early days since the death of the Prophet ﷺ, most of the Muslim community were faithfully sticking to the authentic teachings of the Messenger of Allāh ﷺ. People from the first three generations of Muslims were still alive and were helping to protect the real teachings of Islam from outside influences that may corrupt, adapt or try to change it.

One of the core beliefs of Islam has to do with Allāh and His Speech. As Muslims, we believe that Allāh speaks in a way that befits His Majesty and that speech is an attribute of His. We also believe that the Qur'an is part of Allāh's Speech that He delivered to the Prophet Muhammad ﷺ through the Angel Jibrīl.

Later, a group would emerge that created a new opinion that clashed with the understanding of the Prophet ﷺ and his Companions. This group was called the Muʿtazilah; and they claimed that Allāh did not speak in the Qur'an and it is instead His creation (other humans) who are speaking. The Muʿtazilah themselves knew this belief of theirs was controversial, unpopular and rejected by the Muslims, so they remained underground and hidden from mainstream society.

What does it mean for the Qur'an to be 'created'?

The Qur'an is the word of Allāh and is not created.

What is meant by that is that Allāh, spoke the words of the Qur'an, which Angel Jibrīl heard from Him, and brought down to the Prophet ﷺ, and conveyed to him.

All the attributes of Allāh are uncreated; they are eternal with no beginning. The words of Allāh are among these attributes, and that includes the Qur'an. Therefore, the scholars said that the Qur'an is not created, because it is the words of Allāh.

Regarding people's actions, they are created.

Allāh says: "While Allāh has created you and what you do." (al-Ṣaffāt 37:96).

There are two issues to bear in mind:

- The first is the words of Allāh that He spoke initially, and the Angel Jibrīl heard them from Him, and the Prophet ﷺ conveyed them to us. This is an attribute of Allāh that is not created in its letters and words; the same applies to His voice with which Allāh spoke initially, and Angel Jibrīl heard it from Him.

  All of this comes under the heading of the words of Allāh, nothing of which is created, no matter how it is written, recited or heard.

- The second is the actions of the person, who is the vessel which carries the words of Allāh, so he writes them in a book, reads them and hears them. All that comes from a person and what he does is created.

So, the hand of the person is created, the ink with which he writes is created, the paper on which he writes is created, the person's tongue is created, his voice that belongs to him is created. All of these are vessels in which people carry the word of Allāh and convey it.

Imam al-Bukhārī (Khalq Afʿāl al-ʿIbād 2/70)

They were also in fear of getting caught by the Caliph Hārūn al-Rashīd, who clamped down hard on this group and threatened them with severe consequences if they didn't stop spreading their corrupt beliefs.

One of the main supporters of the Muʿtazilah was a man named Bishr al-Murīsī who would gather and secretly spread this belief to a growing number of followers. While Caliph Hārūn was in power, Bishr acted secretly and, for over 20 years, remained in hiding spreading his beliefs. Caliph Hārūn eventually passed away and his son, al-Amīn took the throne. Bishr remained in hiding until al-Amīn died. Next to take power was al-Amīn's brother, ʿAbdullāh ibn Hārūn, also knowns as al-Ma'mūn.

The Caliph joins the corruption

Sensing that al-Maʿmūn would be easier to convince, Bishr emerged from hiding and together with his growing group, approached the new Caliph and managed to persuade al-Maʿmūn to accept his warped beliefs. This was a major victory for Bishr since al-Maʿmūn was the highest authority in the Muslim world at the time. Initially, al-Maʿmūn was hesitant to impose his new beliefs on all the Muslims since he knew it was a minority opinion and deeply unpopular. Some more time with Bishr, however, changed his mind and he eventually decided to force this corrupt opinion on everybody under his rule.

He first summoned Isḥāq ibn Ibrāhīm, the leader of the police forces, and instructed him to begin an inquisition on people's beliefs about the Qur'an. He began with rounding up seven of the most famous scholars of Baghdad and interrogated them on whether they believed the speech of Allāh was created or not. Under duress, each of the seven scholars eventually agreed to al-Maʿmūn's beliefs and after making these forced statements, they were set free.

Turmoil spreads like wildfire

With the Caliph's police going from house to house and door to door, turmoil engulfed all the major cities of Iraq and then spread into Greater Persia and eventually the Arabian Peninsula too. Secret police flooded the cities and began to detain, interrogate and imprison anybody who didn't openly agree with their beliefs. The prisons of the cities were soon overflowing with innocent people who refused to betray their convictions. Husbands became separated from their wives; children watched their fathers taken away and elderly parents saw their homes torn apart. Caliph al-Maʿmūn stopped at nothing however, and as the strife spread, his eagerness to crush opposing opinions only grew stronger.

The Caliph first wanted to target the scholars and focused his energies on getting them to testify that the corrupt belief (of the Qur'an being created by humans) was correct. He knew that the scholars had power over the people, and they would accept what they were told by their trusted religious authorities. Through violence, threat and torture, most scholars did testify that al-Maʿmūn was correct, and they were therefore spared. During this great upheaval, and while witnessing the bloodshed taking place, two brave men stood against what was happening and rose with courage to declare what al-Maʿmūn was saying was wrong, abhorrent and had no place in Islam. These men were Imam Aḥmad ibn Ḥanbal and his young student, Muḥammad ibn Nūḥ.

When al-Maʿmūn received news of the pair's dissent, he immediately ordered his Chief of Police to find and arrest them. Imam Aḥmad himself recalls: *"I would make duʿa to Allāh that He never shows me the face of al-Maʿmūn, because news came to me that he would say 'If I see Aḥmad, I will cut him up piece by piece.'"*

Not long after however, armed police from the state security services arrived at the homes of Imam Aḥmad and Ibn Nūḥ to arrest them. They were both shackled in heavy chains and being taken to al-Maʿmūn. During the journey, the police were informed of the unexpected news that al-Maʿmūn had just passed away. While still in chains, Imam Aḥmad exhaled and praised Allāh. He believed this would be the end of his ordeal. Unfortunately, the reality couldn't be further from what Imam Aḥmad had hoped in that moment, the true extent of his agony was yet to even begin...

Al-Mu'tasim takes over as Caliph

Another son of Hārūn al-Rashīd (also called Muḥammad) swiftly became the new Caliph, he was known amongst his people as al-Muʿtaṣim. Once he assumed power, al-Muʿtaṣim wasted no time in appointing his chief advisors and chose a man named Aḥmad ibn Abī Du'ād in the most senior position. al-Muʿtaṣim's new advisor was a very staunch believer that the Qur'an was created and wasted no time in ensuring the new Caliph was convinced of the same.

As soon as al-Muʿtaṣim and Ibn Abī Du'ād heard of Imam Aḥmad's resistance to this idea, they immediately summoned them again. For the second time now, Imam Aḥmad and Ibn Nūḥ were arrested and put on a journey to Baghdad. During a perilous and uncertain time, Ibn Nūḥ fell unwell and began to lose consciousness. Fearing his death was near, Ibn Nūḥ wasted no time in his final moments to impart some words of advice to Imam Aḥmad. Struggling as his body was fast deteriorating, Ibn Nūḥ found the strength to tell Imam Aḥmad:

"You are a man who is followed. All of creation have craned their necks to see what you shall do. So fear Allāh and remain patient with whatever Allāh sends your way."

With those parting words, Ibn Nūḥ's soul left his body. Imam Aḥmad, still fettered in chains, felt the sinking realisation that he was now truly alone to endure whatever uncertain fate lay ahead for him.

The imprisonment of Imam Ahmad

Always close to the ear of the Caliph, the advisor Ibn Abī Du'ād had a close eye on Imam Aḥmad and what could be done to him under the Caliph's authority. He advised al-Muʿtaṣim to interrogate Imam Aḥmad and show him no mercy though he was already unwell. True to form, al-Muʿtaṣim followed his advisor's suggestion and had Imam Aḥmad imprisoned in Baghdad during the month of Ramadan.

In the darkness of the dungeon, an ailing Imam Aḥmad was left to languish for two and a half years. The prisons of medieval Arabia were unlike anything you will see today. The cold hard stone floors were boxed in by suffocating walls, with no sunlight or air permitted to enter the stifling cells. Sitting, standing or lying down were all equally agonizing positions to adopt; since, being shackled from his arms to his feet, Imam Aḥmad had almost no free movement. Abandoned and truly alone, Imam Aḥmad's only light in his dark cell would be the fleeting glimmer of candlelight as a guard walked past. In this state, night gave way to day, and day darkened into night, Imam Aḥmad lost sense of time and the cycles of nature altogether.

Meanwhile, amongst Aḥmad's family, worry and distress began to turn into alarm. What would be the fate of Imam Aḥmad and how long would he be left to suffer in prison? Aḥmad's uncle, Isḥāq ibn Ḥanbal, could take it no more and made the perilous journey to meet with the Chief of Police – a fellow named Isḥāq ibn Ibrāhīm.

"I only ask for due process upon my nephew. He has been left to rot in his cell in chains! At least allow Aḥmad to make his case in front of the Caliph himself. He knows his mind and he can defend his views. Bring the scholars of the Muʿtazilah and allow them to face Aḥmad directly, how is there any other way?"

The Chief of Police simply nodded and assured Isḥāq ibn Ḥanbal he would take this matter up with the Caliph. A short time later, al-Muʿtaṣim obliged the request and summoned Imam Aḥmad to court.

Weighed down by his heavy chains, Imam Aḥmad was barely able to walk, falling several times due to exhaustion from the weight of his chains. Everybody stood back and watched this man – so loved among his people – struggle to walk in a straight line. When face to face with the Caliph, he was simply informed that he had one night in a prison cell before the interrogation would begin the following morning.

In the stillness of the night, Imam Aḥmad prayed to his Lord with a level of urgency he had never felt before. He had no idea what lay ahead of him, neither was he able to fully process the torture of what the years had become. Weakened and with nothing but Allāh, Imam Aḥmad prayed for deliverance and awaited what was to come.

The debates begin

The following morning Aḥmad was forcibly dragged in front of the Caliph al-Muʿtaṣim and a waiting audience. There stood a sneering Ibn Abī Du'ād, a host of well-decorated military leaders and the hesitant courtiers of the Caliph. Despite his physical weakness, Imam Aḥmad was the first to open his mouth and request permission to speak. Given the signal, Imam Aḥmad began a full, complete and compelling summary of his position and stated exactly why the belief that the Qur'an was created was unacceptable to Muslims. As Imam Aḥmad spoke, the scholars of the Muʿtazilah grew increasingly agitated and panicked. Following every statement of Imam Aḥmad, they would turn to the Caliph and cry out a variety of rebuffs:

"He is an innovator!"

"He is astray and leads others astray!"

"He is accusing you of disbelief!"

As the scholars of the Muʿtazilah were becoming more hysterical, it became clear to al-Muʿtaṣim that they were only doing so because Imam Aḥmad was defeating them in debate. Once it was the turn of the Muʿtazilah to defend their position, Imam Aḥmad would calmly state after each point:

"O leader of the believers, they have not cited anything from the Qur'an or Sunnah."

This was repeated so many times that the Caliph's scheming advisor Ibn Abī Du'ād finally snapped, *"Are your opinions only taken from the Qur'an and Sunnah?"*

Unaffected by the rage in the question, Imam Aḥmad confidently replied, *"Can Islam stand on anything but the Qur'an and Sunnah?"*

The scholars of the Muʿtazilah were enraged and desperately encouraged al-Muʿtaṣim to execute Imam Aḥmad, claiming he was a heretic and would lead everybody astray if left alive. Having watched how Imam Aḥmad conducted himself, the Caliph was now not so sure. He was hopeful that Imam Aḥmad may eventually accept his beliefs. If this didn't happen however, he at least now fully realised the status of Imam Aḥmad and the importance of having a man like him by his side.

The fierce debate in the court of the Caliph continued in this fashion for the next three days. Following gruelling days of intense questioning and threats, Imam Aḥmad would be returned to his stone cold, dark prison cell to spend his evenings. With little access to food, Imam Aḥmad fasted continuously during this time, only eating the bare minimum to keep him alive. As he attempted to move from the court back to his cell, he was followed closely by a sneering Ibn Abī Du'ād who taunted him with the threat of torture. *"Your fate is in the hands of the Caliph, O Aḥmad ... and I know exactly how to fill the Caliph's ears!"*

Following the third and final day of debate, it became undeniably clear to al-Muʿtaṣim that Imam Aḥmad's views were rock solid, and unlikely to ever change. Rather than entertaining endless discussion, he simply decided to send him back to prison, while he instructed his guards to prepare the apparatus for torture. Punishment was due to begin.

The torture of Imam Ahmad begins

The torture of Imam Aḥmad was well planned, precise and without mercy. An ageing, unwell scholar who was barely surviving on a handful of food was brought to face Ibn Abī Du'ād – who could barely contain his excitement at what was ahead. Between each round of torture, the guards would cry out, *"What do you say with regards to the Qur'an?"* to which Imam Aḥmad would simply reply, *"It is the speech of Allāh."* Enraged, the torturers would respond with another ferocious round of lashing, eventually causing Aḥmad to fall unconscious.

As he witnessed this spectacle, al-Muʿtaṣim even stepped in to negotiate with Imam Aḥmad saying:

"Aḥmad, woe to you! You are killing yourself! Woe to you, accept what I say, and I will personally unshackle you!" Aḥmad did not waver or even honour the Caliph's words with a response, instead he remained resolute. Ignoring the Caliph's attempt to intercede filled al-Muʿtaṣim with an uncontrollable anger. He screamed at his men, *"HURT HIM! May Allāh sever your hand! Hurt him!"*

Emboldened by the Caliph's orders, the torturers threw their arms up and injected more energy into their lashing frenzy until the intensity of the torment eventually caused Imam Aḥmad to fall unconscious.

As he lay lifeless, the panting guards threw down their whips, wiped the sweat from their foreheads and headed over to the limp body of Imam Aḥmad. Unsure whether he was dead or alive, they threw his battered, bruised and bloodied body down on a straw mat. A group of the guards were not happy to stop there however and lifted their steel-rimmed boots and began to stamp on the Imam's motionless body.

At this point, a wave of panic passed over al-Muʿtaṣim as he worried what people would say if he had indeed killed the great Imam Aḥmad. The thought of this terrified al-Muʿtaṣim only because he feared a personal revolt from the masses for taking the life of a much-loved man. Al-Muʿtaṣim ordered his guards to take Imam Aḥmad back to his cell and see if he recovers. As Imam Aḥmad was left with the full consequences of his injuries, Ibn Abī Du'ād took the final opportunity to convince the Caliph to kill Aḥmad once and for all. Al-Muʿtaṣim knew this would be too much of a risky move and instead ordered for Aḥmad to be allowed to recover and then be released.

Reflecting on this moment later, Imam Aḥmad said: *"I was completely out of my senses, when all of a sudden, I woke up inside a room and the chains had been taken off me."*

Fearful of how the public would perceive him, al-Muʿtaṣim had Imam Aḥmad dressed – fresh from torture at his hands – in elaborate royal attire and set him free on the back of an animal. When Imam Aḥmad returned home, the first thing he did was remove the luxurious robes, sell them, and donate the entire proceeds to charity.

Al-Muʿtaṣim soon became consumed with regret for what he had done to Aḥmad, so much so that he would send men to check up on Aḥmad's condition daily. With the passage of time, Imam Aḥmad did indeed slowly recuperate and when his body had regained full strength, he returned to praying in the mosque again. In a cautious recovery, a semblance of normality returned to Imam Aḥmad's life, and he soon took up teaching again. During this time of leading study circles again, the news of al-Muʿtaṣim's death reached Aḥmad.

The rise of a new oppressor: al-Wāthiq

Though many may have assumed that the death of al-Muʿtaṣim would be a welcome relief for Imam Aḥmad, few anticipated what his son, al-Wāthiq, had brewing. The new Caliph was a fierce proponent of the Muʿtazilah creed, even stronger than his father al-Muʿtaṣim, and he wasted no time making this known to everybody. Always close to power, the infamous Ibn Abī Du'ad became a beloved and trusted confidant of al-Wāthiq and, together, they were a force to be reckoned with. The pair wasted no time in torturing and imprisoning anybody whose views opposed theirs, and with no authority higher than them, they caused immense suffering to engulf Baghdad.

Being privy to al-Wāthiq's intentions, the Chief of Police, Isḥāq ibn Ibrāhīm, sent a letter to Imam Aḥmad simply stating: *"The leader of the believers has made mention of your name."* Upon reading these words, Imam Aḥmad understood exactly what he was saying. He had no choice but to go into hiding. This self-imposed exile was very severe on Imam Aḥmad. Not only did he not visit anybody, but he had no visitors himself either. Out of everything he endured, the hardest thing was not being able to pray in the mosque. This situation persisted until news came of al-Wāthiq's death.

The tide turns with al-Mutawakkil

Just as we are promised that with hardship there will be relief, the new Caliph al-Mutawakkil was a believer who honoured the way of the Prophet ﷺ and the understanding of the Companions. Jubilation spread far throughout Baghdad and beyond. Hearing news of the new Caliph, Imam

Aḥmad was finally safe to emerge from hiding. The greatest trial of his life had finally ended, and the Sunnah was victorious. At long last, the people collectively exhaled as they welcomed a new era with Imam Aḥmad firmly revered as a hero for his courage in the face of unspeakable suffering.

Understanding what the previous Caliphs had done, al-Mutawakkil sent a sum of money to Imam Aḥmad, which Imam Aḥmad promptly donated to the poor, along with the lavish bag that the money was sent in. Al-Mutawakkil also invited Aḥmad to dine with him on numerous occasions, however, Aḥmad regularly declined these invitations. When the Caliph continued to insist, Imam Aḥmad finally agreed and was soon stunned to find a huge entourage sent to him from the Caliph. Al-Mutawakkil instructed his staff to prepare a huge banquet sourcing the finest foods and enthusiastically encouraged Imam Aḥmad to partake in the luxuries on offer. Imam Aḥmad, true to form, did not even glance at it.

Being taught patience from a thief

Imam Aḥmad's son, ʿAbdullāh, would recall how his father regularly made mention of the name Abū al-Haytham saying: "I frequently recall my father saying: *'May Allāh have mercy on Abū al-Haytham. May Allāh pardon Abū al-Haytham.'*"

Who was Abu al-Haytham? Imam Aḥmad reveals he met this character while in the middle of extreme torture by lashing. When Imam Aḥmad was being summoned for whipping, he felt a strong tug at his clothes from behind. He looked back to find a man asking, *"Do you know who I am?"* Imam Aḥmad replied that he did not. The questioner then said:

"I am Abū al-Haytham, the free soul and the infamous thief. To date, it is on record that I have received 18,000 lashes, yet I carry on stealing. I have shown patience in obedience to evil and in the cause of worldly gain. So show patience, for you are in obedience to Allāh and in the cause of the religion." [67]

Here was a prolific thief – happily reeling off his list of criminal actions – who had a strong sense of truth and conviction.

Abū al-Haytham's encouragement came at a time when Imam Aḥmad was most in need of it, so Aḥmad never forgot him. Facing abandonment, neglect, isolation and days of lashes followed by nights of agony in a darkened cell, these few words of sincere advice from a great criminal proved to be the balm to

[67] Ibn al-Jawzī, Ṣifat al-Ṣafwa, Dar al-Ghad al-Jadeed, Vol 1, p 485.

soothe Imam Aḥmad's aching self.

Despite his lengthy list of sins and transgressions, Abū al-Haytham didn't hesitate to speak the truth and give the necessary words of encouragement when he saw the opportunity. His words therefore had a strong and shifting effect on Imam Aḥmad and strengthened his heart at a time where he was severely mentally and physically weakened.

This action of his had such sincerity in it that he was never forgotten by Imam Aḥmad. Abū al-Haytham qualified himself as a worthy recipient of the regular duʿa of one of the greatest scholars to ever walk the planet.

Forgiven and forgotten?

After Imam Aḥmad was released from prison, he did what the most noble people often do: he forgave all those who had harmed him.

Aḥmad would recite the verse:

"Let them pardon and overlook. Would you not like that Allāh should forgive you?"

Then he would say: *"How will you benefit if your brother is punished because of you?"* [68]

He made an exception however, and that was for the chief innovators who plotted and planned so much destruction that they could not be given the benefit of the doubt for their actions.

Aḥmad felt so strongly against what the chief innovators had done that he took an oath to Allāh that until the day he died, he would not speak to anyone from the Muslims who gave in to the innovators and testified to their false beliefs. This included his life-long friend and trusted travel companion Yaḥyā ibn Maʿīn. Aḥmad and Yaḥyā had experienced many monumental things in life together and despite Yaḥyā being seven years older, shared a depth of connection that was far beyond mere friendship. Yaḥyā's actions, therefore, stung Aḥmad in a soul-shifting way.

With all this shared history and the pain of knowing what he had done, Yaḥyā one day came to visit Aḥmad. Yaḥyā greeted him with *salām* but Aḥmad did not return the greeting. Yaḥyā then apologised for his outward agreement with the Muʿtazilah and tried to make excuses for his actions, but Aḥmad refused to look his way.

"Aḥmad, there are reasons I did what I did. There's even quotes from our scripture excusing the people who testify to false beliefs when they are under duress.

[68] Ibn Katheer, *Al-Bidāyah wa'l-Nihāyah*, Darrusalam Publications, Vol 10, p 369.

You have to believe me; I had no other choice."

Aḥmad refused to answer.

"I see you do not want to accept any of my excuses," Yaḥyā said aloud as he quietly walked out of Imam Aḥmad's house, sitting on the doorstep in deep grief.

When one of the other house guests came out, Yaḥyā looked up and asked him in hope: *"What did Aḥmad say after I left?"* The guest replied, *"Aḥmad said that the narrations you cited apply to people who are actually being forced, hence Allāh excused them for their actions when they testified to falsehood. He said you weren't under duress; you were merely threatened with the possibility of it and gave in. So Aḥmad doesn't believe what you're saying is valid and thinks you take full responsibility for your choices."*

Upon hearing this, Yaḥyā was heard saying: *"O Aḥmad, say what you wish. May Allāh forgive you, for by Allāh, I have never seen any human being beneath the sky who has a greater understanding of Allāh's religion than you."* [69]

With that, the friendship of Aḥmad and Yaḥyā was laid to rest permanently.

The death of Imam Aḥmad

During the reign of al-Mutawakkil, Aḥmad's ongoing illness grew worse though he continued to fast and refused to abandon this practice. The Caliph regularly sent his own personal physician to Aḥmad to assess, treat and prescribe him medication, however Aḥmad refused to take the medication he was given. Upon returning to the Caliph, his doctor informed him that the cause of Aḥmad's extreme weakness was not so much an illness but a result of his continuous fasting, eating minimal food and intense worship.

Aḥmad also never gave up teaching others as well as pursuing his own learning. He would say: *"I will pursue knowledge until the day I enter my grave."*

Someone once saw Imam Aḥmad carrying his pen and paper, so he asked him, *"Father of ʿAbdullāh, you still carry around your pen and paper despite having become the Imam of the Muslims?"*

Imam Aḥmad replied: *"With the inkpot to the graveyard."* [70]

Al-Marrūdhī once asked Aḥmad, *"How are you this morning?"* His response gives an accurate depiction of Aḥmad's disposition in life.

He replied: *"How is the morning of a person who has a Lord who demands from him the obligations, and a Prophet ﷺ who demands the application of his teachings, and two angels who demand that he corrects his deeds, and a soul that demands its desires, and the Shayṭān who demands the committing of sins,*

[69] Ibn Abi Ya'la, *Tabaqāt al-Hanābilah,* Dar al-Marefah, Beirut, 2004, Vol 1, p 404.
[70] Ibn al-Jawzī, *Manāqib Aḥmad Ibn Ḥanbal,* p 31.

and the Angel of Death who eagerly awaits to claim his soul, and a family who demands expenditure?" [71]

With his body slowly losing strength, Aḥmad knew that the time of his soul's departure was near. Too weak to move, he indicated to his family that he wished to perform *wuḍū'.* As they brought a bowl of water near, he gestured to his hands and asked that they wash the areas between his fingers thoroughly, in keeping with the Sunnah. It was just before noon on a Friday in Rabī ʿal-Awwal 241 AH when, freshly in *wuḍū'*, the blessed soul of this extraordinary human being returned to its Creator.

During his life when Imam Aḥmad would be taunted by the Muʿtazilah for his beliefs, he would simply respond: *"Say to the innovators, the funeral procession shall determine who is upon the truth."*

His intuition – as always – proved to be true.

It was estimated that his funeral was attended by 800,000 people. Other narrations say that it was closer to 1.3 million people, while others put the number at 2.5 million people.

ʿAbd al-Wahhāb al-Warrāq said: *"We do not know of a funeral procession – whether during Islam or pre-Islam – that was larger than that of Imam Aḥmad."* [72]

When the chief of the innovators who tortured, imprisoned and delighted in the suffering of Imam Aḥmad – Ibn Abī Du'ād – died, his funeral was largely boycotted and barely attended.

In this is a proof of the strength of one man's impact upon the hearts of all those who knew him and knew of him. The legacy of Imam Aḥmad remains as powerful today as it was during his lifetime. He toiled his entire life in the service of Allāh and will forever go down as the great defender of the Sunnah, standing against the tide in truth and courage.

---

[71] Ibn Abi Ya'la, *Tabaqāt al-Hanābilah,* Dar al-Marefah, Beirut, 2004, Vol 1, p 57.

[72] Ibn Katheer, *Al-Bidāyah wa'l-Nihāyah*, Darrusalam Publications, Vol 10, p 376.

Lessons we can learn

We prepare for the things we love

Even as a youth, when Imam Aḥmad was beginning his studies, he would wake up hours before dawn so he could be dressed, present and as close to the teacher as possible. He woke up so early in fact, that his mother was concerned for his lack of rest and would sometimes physically hold him back from leaving so early.

We all make time for the things in life we are passionate about. In fact, where you most spend your time often says a lot about your priorities. When we think we don't have time for something, it's not because there aren't enough hours in the day, but simply because we have not prioritised it enough above everything else. Our important life goals will require some level of preparation – whether that is practical, psychological, emotional or even financial. Those who prepare and set themselves on the path to achieving great things with a strong intention will find that Allāh easily throws open the doors of opportunity for them. Nothing worth having in life is going to come without exertion, effort and hard work. Just as Imam Ahmad woke up hours ahead of his class in anticipation, you too can lay down the steps to achieving what you want.

Humility will enrich every aspect of your life

When we think of humility, many of us associate being humble with having a lack of pride or ego. Though this is a branch of humility (and an extremely important one), Imam Aḥmad shows us that humility is a holistic trait that touches many aspects of our character and actions. Imam Aḥmad showcased his quiet humility in several different ways. Living in a society where tribal affiliations were taken note of, Imam Aḥmad never felt superior for being an Arab or made mention of this to any of his students or associates. When he was asked to make du'a for a lady suffering paralysis, his humility led him to return the request with, *"I am more in need of her du'a than she is of mine!".* When the sheer love of his students caused them to supplicate, *"May Allāh reward you for everything you have done for Islam!",* Imam Aḥmad immediately became uncomfortable and agitated, changing around the du'a as he saw more fit: *"Rather, may Allāh reward Islam for everything it has done for me."* When his fame began to grow and spread in his lifetime, Imam Aḥmad remained extremely wary and cautious of ever entertaining his high status amongst the people.

Imam Aḥmad therefore showcased all the different faces of humility. He was at pains to remind himself and others of his weak and needy status in the sight of Allāh. He had adopted humility as such an engrained mindset that you can easily observe how it filtered into all his interactions. Through his character, Imam Aḥmad shows us that genuine humility is not an outward show or a few carefully selected words, but rather a state of mind, heart and soul.

It is always safest to tread with caution

Coupled with humility, one of the other defining traits of Imam Aḥmad was his caution towards all his affairs. He considered and thought through all his actions and never behaved on a whim or moment of passion. Like his humility, Imam Aḥmad applied his sense of caution across all aspects of his life. He was cautious to apply all the knowledge he acquired, he was cautious in speaking without certain knowledge and he was cautious about his reputation growing and him feeling proud or arrogant about this.

Caution is something that will never let us down. Stepping back to assess our state of mind before we act will often save us from many difficulties later on. It takes self-control, discipline and an ability to supress our egotistical inclinations to become self-aware people. Taking a cautious attitude to our actions will save us from much harm, humiliation and regret.

Gather pearls of wisdom... even from a criminal

For as long as he lived, Imam Aḥmad never stopped remembering or supplicating for Abū al-Haytham, to the point that even his grown son learnt of his name and story. Abū al-Haytham was a prolific thief and a shameless criminal, yet his convictions of right and wrong were solid. People are complicated and though outwardly it might appear that they have no benefit to bring you, they may be able to present you with wisdom, benefit and perspective that you never imagined.

At a time where Imam Aḥmad was feeling most vulnerable and overcome, the brief encounter with Abū al-Haytham strengthened his heart and boosted his resolve to keep going and remain patient in the face of unimaginable suffering. Abū al-Haytham teaches us that we should take good advice wherever it comes from, and never judge someone as not having anything to offer you. Abū al-Haytham was not a 'match' for Imam Aḥmad in terms of knowledge, character or actions – yet he was just the person Imam Aḥmad needed to hear from and he delivered the exact words, at the exact time and in the exact way that benefitted him most. Keep your heart and mind open, as sometimes the most profound lessons in life can come from the unlikeliest of places or people!

It takes bravery to stand alone against an ocean

The greatest trial of Imam Aḥmad's life was undoubtedly resisting the spread of the Muʿtazilah and their false beliefs. This took up almost two decades of his life and left Imam Aḥmad an old, physically sick and weakened man. When we look back on his life, however, a significant portion of Imam Aḥmad's legacy rests on how he stood firm and resolute, when all those around him were crumbling.

Nobody remembers those who succumbed to testifying to false beliefs and even the chief innovators have been forgotten in the annals of history. What secured Imam Aḥmad's reputation as a defender of the Sunnah was his dedication to the truth, even when it cost him everything. Most of us will never be in such an extreme position of persecution and injustice as Imam Aḥmad was, however, we will have all experienced the feeling of swimming against the tide. It may seem like, as believers, we are distinct from the mainstream when we stay loyal to our principles. This requires conviction, bravery and patience. Often what is popular and promoted amongst the masses isn't what is healthiest for our soul. In this way, the believers will always be "strangers" in a world that is geared around only maximising pleasure, not considering consequences, and living in and for the moment. Imam Aḥmad's bravery didn't come from thin air, it was laid on a firm foundation of sure knowledge and strong spiritual practice. The more we learn and know of Allāh's dīn, the more courage we will unearth to stand by it.

The truth will always make itself known eventually

Since the death of Ibn Nūḥ, Imam Aḥmad was used to being alone. Despite the pressure of the Caliphs, the Chief of Police and the sheer number of scholars who were testifying to false beliefs, Imam Aḥmad never wavered in his position. Instead, he confidently remarked that the funeral procession would reveal who is on the truth or not. What he meant by this is that the truth will eventually be made clear to people, and falsehood – by its nature – will perish.

Often, we worry, panic and become anxious when we are in a position of weakness or an oppressive situation. We want our side of the story to be heard immediately and swift justice to be enacted. Though there is nothing wrong with this, we must also sometimes accept that we might not experience that satisfaction when we want to. Instead, Allāh Himself will reveal – through His perfect timing and in His perfect way – who is on the side of truth and will vindicate all those who have been treated unjustly. Sometimes you don't need to fight so hard since you have a Lord that will fight on your behalf. What He decrees as the outcome will be greater than anything you could have done yourself. To truly understand this, requires us to stay patient and keep steadfast.

A Final Thought

Looking back and looking forward

The Four Imams were regular people like you and me, who achieved extraordinary heights in their life. Each of their stories have extremely noteworthy points of difference, as well as **strong commonalities that bind them together.** The Four Imams are not legends or folklore, they are not superheroes in capes or celestial beings. **They were living, breathing embodiments of the things we can achieve when we set a sincere vision for ourselves** and apply every effort to achieve it.

You will see from their lives that the Imams encountered every spectrum of human experience (and more!) that we do today. Some of them were born with all the odds stacked against them, others were born in stable, wealthy families. Some had easy access to scholarship, others had to struggle to find the people they needed to learn from. Some had an air of awe around them, while others were down-to-earth and extremely approachable by the people.

All of them faced and **dealt with challenges that came from the state, community, friendships, family, and their very own soul.** Within the variety of experiences that the Four Imams had, we can draw a wealth of lessons that directly apply to our own lives here and now. That is because the basic needs and behaviours of human beings do not change – whether they lived 1000 years ago or today. **The names, places and dates will be different but fundamentally, the things that make a life worth living remain the same.**

The Four Imams all experienced extreme struggles and great victories. Some struggled through severe poverty and hardship, whilst others explored new and exciting worlds as they travelled as wide as the world is vast. As you read through the stories, you will have noticed particular themes reoccur and these are the aspects of human nature that will always remain consistent among us. **All the Imams cautioned heavily against seeking fame and loving to hear yourself being praised.** They all went to great lengths to preserve their sincerity and keep Allāh's pleasure as their only goal.

They all focused on **learning the manners of being a student of knowledge before beginning formal study of the religion.** This is because they understood that without a good character, anything they learnt would be futile. Teachers with bad character would drive students away from their knowledge and not be able to guard themselves from feeling proud, smug or arrogant because of what they knew. **The Imams were also closely involved with the affairs of their people.** They dealt directly with their community daily and had a strong grasp of what the issues within their society were. The **knowledge they were acquiring was not meant to be preserved in elite, ivory towers but practically applied to improve the lives of the people around them** – whether that was a drunk neighbour or an elderly, paralysed woman. The different schools of thought that each Imam created are a source of strength to our intellectual tradition. They are never meant to be treated as rivals to one another or different 'brands' of Islam to follow. The spirit and practice of the Four Imams demonstrates this strongly as they always behaved as allies, friends and helpers to one another for the sake of Allāh. The madhabs aid unity and not division.

Though the Imams lived many years ago, **Islamic scholarship is still active and alive in communities around the world** today. Islam has a beautiful history, a flourishing present and an incredible future ahead too. **Scholarship therefore is a living breathing tradition, and this continues through all ages.** You will most likely be able to find teachers and scholars closer than you think if you look for them. Every society, in every country will have people who have dedicated themselves to Islamic knowledge and these are the people worth seeking out.

Don't think, however, that everybody must become an Imam or leader like these people. There is a role for everybody in society. Alongside the Imams were their students, supporters, well-wishers, and people bringing practical benefit to the cause of goodness in whichever way they were inclined. Don't narrow the ways you can contribute to your community, there is a path available for everyone.

Each of **the Imams were unique, individual characters too.** Imam al-Shāfiʿī had a strong love for language and immersed himself in the endless ocean of

Arabic and its many fields. Imam Abū Ḥanīfah redefined what our attitude to wealth and conducting ourselves in business should look like. Imam Mālik was firmly rooted in the scholarship and traditional learning of Madinah, heartland of the Companions. Imam Aḥmad stood bravely and defiantly against decades of oppression, political upheaval and the entire country, as he knew it, thrown into turmoil. **Each of them harnessed their skills to meet the challenges of their day in the most appropriate, effective and exemplary way.** The differences in their character show us that each of us have unique gifts and **every one of our God-given attributes are gifted to us with a set purpose.** It is only up to us to tap into it and use it for the betterment of our own souls and the people around us.

The Four Imams leave behind endless lessons, points of reflection and incidents to delight, awe and humble us. Their legacy has stood the test of time, while ours is still in the works. Just as we look upon these scholars before us, we must truly believe and trust each of us has the potential to lay down a legacy of our own – however that looks for each of us. **Allāh has put you on this earth with the personality you have, the loved ones around you, the place you were born, and the opportunities in your life for a clear purpose: for your soul to reach its full potential.** As we have learnt from those before us, let us look towards our own future.

Consider, ponder and reflect: what kind of legacy would you like to leave behind?